Fred Gipson at Work

Fred Gipson at Work

By Glen E. Lich

Texas A&M University Press
College Station

First Edition

The following publishers have given permission to quote extensively from Fred Gipson's copyrighted works: Harper's, for *Recollection Creek*, copyright 1944, 1945, 1946, 1947, 1948, and 1955; *Hound-Dog Man*, copyright 1949; *The Home Place*, copyright 1950; *The Trail-Driving Rooster*, copyright 1955; *Old Yeller*, copyright 1956; *Cowhand*, copyright 1958; *Savage Sam*, copyright 1962; *Little Arliss*, copyright 1978; and *Curly and the Wild Boar*, copyright 1979. All early copyrights renewed by T. Beck Gipson. Houghton Mifflin, for *Fabulous Em pire*, copyright 1946 and copyright renewed 1974 by T. Beck Gipson. The University of Texas Press, for *Big Bend*, copyright 1952 and 1973, and "*The Cow Killers*", copyright 1956. Eakin Press, for *Before Old Yeller*, copyright 1980.

Chapter Five and part of Chapter Six are reprinted from *Cross-Timbers Review*.

Frontispiece: Fred Gipson (photograph by Ellison Studio, Austin, courtesy T. Beck Gipson)

The paper used in this book meets the minimum requirements of the American National Standard for Permanence of Paper for Printed Library Materials, Z39.48-1984. Binding materials have been chosen for durability. ♾

Library of Congress Cataloging-in-Publication Data
Lich, Glen E., 1948–
Fred Gipson at work / by Glen E. Lich.
p. cm.
Includes bibliographical references.
ISBN 0-89096-424-6
1. Gipson, Fred, 1908– —Criticism and interpretation. 2. Texas in literature. I. Title.
PS3513.I79Z75 1990
813'.54—dc20 89-39876
CIP

To Jambalaya,
Uncle Poos,
and Honey Bee

Contents

Preface

This book on the work of Fred Gipson explores the extent to which the novels and histories of the most widely read twentieth-century Texas writer before Larry McMurtry project an alter ego of mainstream America. Searching for what Leon Edel calls the "figure in the reverse of the tapestry," the volume traces changes in Gipson's conception of the region and argues that Gipson's histories and fiction look simultaneously to the past and to the future and thus reveal both memory and aspiration.[1] And citing parallels in the lives and writing of other Texas writers and public figures, the study suggests a broad regional ethology.

Fred Gipson's novels have been translated into many languages, from German and Swedish to Turkish and Japanese. Several became film successes. One sold more copies than any other novel by a native Texan. A. C. Greene said Gipson "came very near to writing a Texas Huckleberry Finn." Sam Henderson's assessment was that Gipson "made the term Southwest literature legitimate and meaningful" and "accomplished the rare but admirable feat of turning the bits and pieces of folklore into myth."[2] Walter Prescott Webb admitted that Gipson's work might outlast *The Great Plains* and *The Great Frontier.* And Gipson's historical writings reveal intricate relationships between landscape and myth, between the small and the large worlds, between symbol and health. Gipson was "a kind of tragic figure," his friend Tom Lea recalled, but "a hell of a nice guy."[3] The older he grew, however, the more Gipson opposed the world. As his bitterness increased, his writings turned more and more toward youth, for whom he still maintained hope. The happy endings that may seem to weaken the novels actually underscore his moral intent. He was capable also of devastating endings, as the biographies he wrote show. Too many things could go wrong if one lived long enough. His own life proved his fear.

This criticism of Gipson's works and life within broad social and cultural contexts is the necessarily impressionistic outlook that Leon Edel describes as "the biographer's vision of his subject."[4] Readers who want plain facts, so to speak, must first turn to Mike Cox's *Fred Gipson: Texas Storyteller* or to Sam Henderson's monograph *Fred Gipson. Fred Gipson at Work*, ranging beyond those but dependent upon them for their solid core of biographical detail, is organized around Gipson's writings, because autobiographical qualities in his books mark the rise and fall of Gipson's creative fortune.

Chapter 1, entitled "The World of Comanche Creek, 1908–1933," introduces the patterns, values, symbols, and structures of Gipson's childhood world. "'One Step Further,' 1933–1937," is based on Gipson's essays and newspaper writings at the University of Texas, edited by C. Richard King in *Before Old Yeller*. This chapter closes out the 1930s and moves into the 1940s. "'Gifts of God That Were Free to All,' 1944–1949," takes its title from *Recollection Creek* (conceived between 1944 and 1948, published in 1955), a watershed from which Gipson's other novels flow. This chapter, spanning the rest of the forties, also discusses a biography entitled *Fabulous Empire* (1946) and a novel favored by Gipson himself, *Hound-Dog Man* (1949), later a movie. "'A Good Dream,' 1950–1953," focuses on *The Home Place* (1950), from which the chapter title is taken, and includes besides this novel, later filmed as *The Return of the Texan*, two biographies—*Big Bend* (1952) and *Cowhand* (1953); the chapter covers the first half of the fifties.

"'Memories Are Long,' 1956," is an essay on "*The Cow Killers*" (1956), a collection of documentary vignettes. Gipson's most forceful writing, this book could have led him in a new direction.

"'A Sort of Double Meaning,' 1955–1965," surveys the juveniles, dominated by *Old Yeller* (1956) and including *The Trail-Driving Rooster* (1955), *Savage Sam* (1962), and two posthumous juveniles: *Little Arliss* (1978) and *Curly and the Wild Boar* (1979). Walt Disney made movies based on two of these novels. The last chapter, "'Peace Is a Dream,' 1965–1973," assesses Gipson's place as a writer of picaresque, pastoral, western, and juvenile fantasies which reveal an increasingly hostile stance toward a changing world.

Acknowledgments

Texas is a dichotomy of "world capital" and "howling wilderness," in Katherine Anne Porter's words. Left alone, such oppositions generate power, making Texas at once the "most American of places" and a part of the developing Third World, giving the state an inclination that John Graves describes as "backward progress." To both Porter and Graves, I acknowledge the debt of a literary heritage.

For encouragement to study that heritage and to write a book which combines my interests in community and regional studies, biography and literature, landscape and culture, I thank Betsy Colquitt, Jim Corder, Fred Erisman, David Vanderwerken, Harry Opperman, Bob Frye, and Neil Daniel.

Joe B. Frantz, Terry Jordan, Gilbert Jordan, A. C. Greene, Frank Wardlaw, Martha Dobie, Elroy Bode, Lou Rodenberger, and Bill Leftwich offered insights, advice, readings, and various sorts of assistance. The work of Sam Henderson and Mike Cox gave me numerous advantages. The staff of the Humanities Research Center at the University of Texas at Austin made Fred Gipson materials available. Permission to use these materials was granted by Thomas Beckton Gipson of Kerrville. The Gipson family gave me access to Fred Gipson's private library, to family memorabilia, and to the old Gipson haunts in "the world of Comanche Creek."

My appreciation goes also to Texas Christian University and Schreiner College for substantial support that allowed me to linger in solitude with these ideas, and to Kay Satchell, Mary Ann Parker, Anabel Rivera, and Leslie Nichols for letting me change my mind.

And while I was off on the mesa of high adventure, my wife Lera held our world together. This volume is dedicated to our children with the wish that they too measure their lives with "color, excitement, and high drama," as we have had the good luck to measure ours.

Chronology

Chronology source credits are given in the Notes section.

	1899	Beck and Emma Gipson, Fred Gipson's parents, move from Hunt County, Texas, to Mason County, arriving in November.
Population of Texas: 3,048,710; 17.1 percent urban, 82.9 percent rural.	1900	
Spindletop initiates the oil boom in Texas.	1901	
	1908	Fred Gipson is born on February 7 in a small cabin at the Gooch place, on Comanche Creek. He has four older sisters, and his parents are poor cotton farmers.
The Texas Agricultural Extension Service begins to offer scientific services to farmers and ranchers.	1912	
	1915	Gipson begins school in a two-story sandstone building across Comanche Creek in the town of Mason. He nearly loses his life at a gathering in nearby Katemcy.

U.S. enters World War I.	1917	
	1922	Gipson shoots his first buck with an octagonal barrel .30-.30 Winchester rifle. The fourteen-year-old strikes a field laborer with a hoe, cutting him and knocking him out.
Cotton prices drop 400 percent after the war boom.	1920s	
Dorothy Scarborough publishes *The Wind* (1925).	1922–26	Gipson attends high school in Mason, publishes his first short story (in the school annual), and competes in literary and declamation contests.
	1926	Gipson enrolls for a year in Draughon's Business College in San Antonio.
	1927	Gipson works for Ned Polk on a goat drive from Edwards County to the James River in Mason County, the site of some of the last trail drives.
	1928	Gipson works for the county as a mule skinner on a road repair crew and operates the first motorized road machinery in Mason County.
J. Frank Dobie publishes *A Vaquero of the Brush Country.* Jimmie Rodgers moves to Kerrville, and the town becomes a center for country and western music.	1929	
Population of Texas rises to 5,824,715; 41 percent urban, 59 percent rural.	1930	

J. Frank Dobie publishes *Coronado's Children* and Katherine Anne Porter publishes *Flowering Judas.*		
Walter Prescott Webb writes *The Great Plains.*	1931	The Depression worsens, and the Gipson family suffers. Fred Gipson and his father secure jobs as day-laborers. Fred Gipson threatens to beat a road crew supervisor in order to get back pay due him and his father.
	1933	Gipson enrolls at the University of Texas. He meets Joe Small, journalism student.
Big Bend National Park is created.	1935	Fred Gipson's stories begin to appear in the *Daily Texan.*
	1936	Gipson wins a writing contest judged by J. Frank Dobie. "Hard-Pressed Sam" is published in the January issue of *Southwest Review.* He is elected president of the local chapter of Sigma Delta Chi, the national journalism society, and starts a regular column in the *Daily Texan.* On October 19, his father Beck Gipson dies in Mason at age 64.
	1937	Gipson starts working on the *Corpus Christi Caller-Times,* published by Grady Kinsolving. On February 7, his first byline story appears. He becomes a roving reporter in Corpus Christi and on the road. His stories become more and more personal.
J. Frank Dobie writes *Apache Gold and Yaqui Silver.* Kather-	1939	In the summer, Gipson meets and courts Tommie Wynn of San Angelo.

ine Anne Porter publishes *Pale Horse, Pale Rider.*		The REA builds electric lines in Mason County.
Population of Texas: 6,414,824; 45.4 percent urban, 54.6 percent rural. This is the last time the rural exceeds the urban population. There are 516,000 occupied farm dwellings.	1940	On January 23, Gipson marries Tommie Wynn in San Angelo. They take a wedding trip to Monterrey, Mexico. In June, Gipson is fired from his newspaper job and moves back to Mason. *Gone with the Wind* is shown for the first time in Mason. On October 29, Fred and Tommie Gipson's first son, Phillip Michael, is born.
J. Frank Dobie publishes *The Longhorns.* The U.S. enters World War II.	1941	Early in the year, Joe Small sets himself up as Bill Manning, Literary Agent of the Southwest. Gipson sells to the pulps western stories based on authentic episodes like the Hoo-Doo War in Mason County. He works up to a rate of a penny per word. Small and Gipson try to peddle a syndicated newspaper column, "Around Our Place."
	1942	By August, Fred Gipson is earning enough money to build a two-room house on eleven acres deeded to him and Tommie by his mother.
	1943	The Gipsons move to Austin and live across from the Small family. Gipson receives a five-hundred-dollar check from *Collier's* for "Lonesome Man."
Katherine Anne Porter publishes *The Leaning Tower.*	1944	Gipson moves his family back to their two-room cottage without electricity in Mason County. "My Kind of Man" appears in the *Southwest Review* and is sold to *Reader's Digest* for sixteen hundred dollars. He adds two rooms and a bath to the cottage and gives in to Tommie's pleas for a second child.

		Gipson starts on a novel, but it progresses slowly as he does bits and pieces that later go into *Recollection Creek*. In November Gipson meets Col. Zack Miller, boss of the famed 101 Wild West Show and 101 Ranch in Oklahoma, in Kerr County at the Raigorodsky Ranch, where Gipson collects a thousand pages of notes, the basis of *Fabulous Empire*.
World War II ends.	1945	Gipson completes the manuscript draft of the Miller story. "Melon Patch Killing," a story based on a J. Marvin Hunter sketch, is sold to *Southwest Review*. On June 17, Thomas Beckton Gipson, the second son, is born. Gipson goes to New York to meet people at *Reader's Digest* and Houghton Mifflin. He also meets Maurice Crain, a native of New Mexico and a boyhood resident of the Texas Panhandle who became Gipson's literary agent. Crain's wife, Annie Laurie Williams, became Gipson's first movie agent. Mason incorporates.
	1946	April through October brings health and financial problems. Gipson sells another story to *Reader's Digest*. In September, *Fabulous Empire* is published, and Gipson returns to the first novel, which he is calling "Clipped Wings," later known as *Hound-Dog Man*. Mason schools begin consolidating.
	1947	*Hound-Dog Man* is sent to Maurice Crain, who forwards it to Houghton Mifflin, where the manuscript is held for nine months. Eventually the edi-

tors suggest revisions which Fred Gipson refuses to consider. Crain circulates the manuscript to other New York publishers.

The first television station in the state, WBAP-TV, begins broadcasting in Fort Worth.	1948	Donald Day is instrumental in securing Fred Gipson a position with the *Denver Post* as a roving editor and as a feature writer for its Sunday magazine, *Rocky Mountain Empire.* In February, the Gipsons depart for Durango, Colorado. By summer, they decide to return to Texas. In June "Clipped Wings" is accepted by John Fischer, editor-in-chief of Harpers, upon advice of assistant Evan Thomas. The book is accepted by Book-of-the-Month Club as a dual selection with *Cheaper by the Dozen,* with a guarantee to Gipson of twenty-five thousand dollars. British rights to *Hound-Dog Man* sell, but the title is changed first to *Cotton Kenny* and eventually to *Circle Round the Wagons.* The Gipson family drives to New York city to visit with the Crains and people at Harpers. A local bank denies Gipson a loan for a new car. Gipson briefly meets John Steinbeck. Gipson refuses invitations to move to New York; for this decision he is praised by Elizabeth Stover of the *Southwest Review.* In August, Gipson's "My Kind of Man" is anthologized in a writing and composition textbook.
The Farm-to-Market Road system is extended throughout the state.	1949	*Hound-Dog Man* appears as a "Harper Find" book and secures extensive coverage in *Book-of-the-Month-Club News* and in reviews. Between 1951 and 1963, the novel would be pub-

lished in German, French, Italian, and Japanese editions. McMurray Bookshop in Dallas holds an autograph party for Gipson. Gipson wins the McMurray Bookshop Award. Gipson goes into a half-year depression and writes "A Town of Beer and Sorrow" for *Southwest Review.* He works on a new novel that fails; Harpers and Crain feel that "The Devil to Pay" is not a good book to follow *Hound-Dog Man.*

Population of Texas rises to 7,711,194; 62.7 percent urban, 37.3 percent rural. This is the first census in which the urban residents outnumber rural dwellers in Texas.

1950 Evan Thomas visits Mason in January and a new novel is mapped out. In April, the Gipsons produce "The Home Place," and the manuscript is accepted by Harpers. In July, People's Book Club accepts *The Home Place* for its December selection, promising to print 100,000 copies. In September, *The Home Place* appears from Harpers. Twentieth Century Fox buys movie rights to *The Home Place* for $27,500. In October, Gipson makes an autograph tour of Texas. Gipson starts conservation work on his farm. In December, *The Home Place* is on the *New York Times* bestseller list and rights are sold to publishers in Great Britain and Germany.

1951 From January through the spring Gipson looks for new writing subjects and starts "The Way of Jesse Gentry," intended as a sequel to *Hound-Dog Man.* Six of Gipson's old *Denver Post* stories are selected for an anthology to be published by Doubleday called *Rocky Mountain Empire.* Filming starts on *The Return of the Texan,* as *The Home Place* was retitled. "The

Way of Jesse Gentry" is completed but rejected by Harpers. Frank Wardlaw, director of the University of Texas Press, commissions Fred Gipson to collaborate with J. O. Langford on what is to become *Big Bend,* completed at the insistence of Henry B. Du Pont.

Walter Prescott Webb publishes *The Great Frontier.* J. Frank Dobie publishes *The Mustangs.*	1952	*Big Bend: A Homesteader's Story* is published. Gipson finds himself in a literary depression. *The Return of the Texan,* a movie based on *The Home Place,* premieres in Austin. The drought in Texas, which worsens until 1957, inhibits Gipson's conservation plans. Numerous stories are rejected.
	1953	Gipson and Joe Small start *True West,* a pulp magazine of nonfiction western stories. *Cowhand,* Gipson's biography of Ed ("Fat") Alford, is published with good reviews and modest sales. A television play based on "My Kind of Man" is aired on CBS on September 24. Tommie Gipson miscarries a baby girl. Gipson works on "Trail-Driving Rooster," which is accepted by Harpers.
	1954	*Trail-Driving Rooster* is completed. Gipson works on a novel developed from some of his earlier short stories; in May, Harpers accepts this manuscript, "Recollection Creek." In summer the Gipsons take a two-month trip over the western United States collecting material for a travel book. In the fall, "The Road Leads West" is rejected by Harpers.
	1955	*Recollection Creek* and *Trail-Driving*

Rooster are published, with modest sales. Television rights are sold to the short story "Brush Roper." Gipson goes to Hollywood as a screenwriter, and on November 24 the weekly television series begins. Gipson begins working on a new juvenile about a boy and his dog.

1956 The manuscript, "Big Yeller Dog," is completed in under three months and receives an overwhelmingly positive reception from Harpers. Before the galleys are finished Gipson has been promised thirty-five thousand dollars for publication rights. Gipson changes to a new firm, the H. N. Swanson Agency, to negotiate movie rights to his novels. By May, Gipson is suffering from relentless back pain. In June, Walt Disney agrees to produce *Old Yeller* and pays fifty thousand dollars for the rights. Between 1958, when the movie was released, and 1973, *Old Yeller* would be published in German, Norwegian, Danish, Swedish, French, Spanish, Italian, Czech, Turkish, and Japanese editions. In collaboration with Bill Leftwich, who illustrated the volume, Gipson writes the text to "'The Cow Killers.'" At the Texas Institute of Letters, Gipson receives the $100 Cokesbury Bookstore Award for *Trail-Driving Rooster* and the $250 McMurrey Bookshop Award for *Recollection Creek*. In August, Gipson goes to California to write the script for *Old Yeller.* He develops a serious ulcer which is worsened by his chronic drinking. In November, *"The Cow Killers"* is published by the University of Texas Press.

1957 The drought in Texas ends. The filming of *Old Yeller* begins. Gipson and Joe Small go on a long fishing trip to Mexico. In December, pre-premiere showings of *Old Yeller* are held in San Angelo and in Mason.

1958 *Old Yeller* opens and rapidly becomes a box office success. The winter in Texas is wet, assuring Gipson that the drought is over. Three of Gipson's short stories are rejected, and Gipson goes to Hollywood again, this time to write the script to the movie *Hound-Dog Man*, which is released in November. Changes in the story of Blackie Scantling incite Gipson to uncontrollable rages, and Tommie Gipson arbitrates all further revisions; the movie receives poor reviews. Mason celebrates its centennial year.

1959 The Gipsons purchase from the Reichenau family, but do not yet move to, a 320-acre "ranch" on the Llano River.

Population of Texas: 9,579,677; 75 percent urban, 25 percent rural. The number of farms drops to 227,000—less than half the number in 1940.

1960 In February Gipson goes to Galveston for shock treatments for acute depression. Gipson is nominated as president of the Texas Institute of Letters. Gipson makes improvements on his new land and his health likewise improves. In the summer, he plans a sequel to *Old Yeller*. Soon thereafter, Gipson is jailed for assault and battery after kicking a neighbor whose pig farm fouled the atmosphere at the old Gipson home place. Brother-in-law Ned Polk intervenes to avert the outbreak of worse hostilities.

Larry McMurtry publishes *Horseman, Pass By.*	1961	The first draft of *Savage Sam* is completed in January, and the revision is finished by May. Between 1963 and 1972, the novel would be published in Danish, Swedish, German, and French editions. Disney buys the movie rights for $25,000. In October, Gipson goes to Hollywood to begin the screenwriting for *Savage Sam* at $1,250 a week. Gipson plans a new home on the Reichenau place on the Llano.
	1962	The book, *Savage Sam,* is released in February. In April, the movie script for it is completed and Gipson gladly returns to Mason. In late spring, Mike and Beck Gipson find the Gipson family dog, the prototype for Savage Sam, clubbed to death behind the Gipson home. Several days later the older son, Mike Gipson, a student at the University of Texas, commits suicide in Austin.
John F. Kennedy is assassinated, and Lyndon B. Johnson becomes president on November 22. Larry McMurtry publishes *Leaving Cheyenne.*	1963	The movie version of *Savage Sam* premieres in Mason in June. In August, Tommie Gipson leaves Fred and returns to San Angelo. Walter Prescott Webb is killed in an automobile accident.
"Red-neck rock" music develops in Austin.	1964	Tommie and Fred Gipson are divorced.
	1965	Gipson's mother dies in Mason, and J. Frank Dobie dies in Austin.
Larry McMurtry publishes *The Last Picture Show.*	1966	Gipson writes a foreword to his sister's history of Mason County; his tone is hostile and self-pitying.

	1967	Gipson's surviving son, Beck Gipson, marries Carolyn Cook on July 7. Fred Gipson marries Angelina Torres from Mexico on December 17. Sam H. Henderson publishes a monograph, *Fred Gipson.*
	1968	Gipson and Angelina are divorced. *Little Arliss* is started. Daughter-in-law Carolyn lives with him while son Beck is in Vietnam.
Population of Texas rises to 11,196,730. Four-fifths of all Texans live in urban areas; some 214,000 farms are enumerated, of which only 152,440 are occupied.	1970	Gipson is named a fellow of the Texas Institute of Letters.
Willie Nelson, Waylon Jennings, Jerry Jeff Walker, and Ray Hubbard become leaders of progressive country music.	1973	Gipson travels to Mexico to find a secretary and companion. He dies in his Mason County home on August 14 and is buried on August 17 at the State Cemetery in Austin. His close friend Frank Wardlaw, founder of two university presses in Texas, delivers the eulogy.
	1978	*Little Arliss* is published.
	1979	*Curly and the Wild Boar* is published.

Fred Gipson at Work

CHAPTER ONE

The World of Comanche Creek 1908–1933

The Hill Country of Texas pervades every page of Fred Gipson's novels. Largely autobiographical, the six novels published during his lifetime, the two posthumously published novels, and four other book-length works map a coherent personal geography of a magic mountain raised above the world below, a place where German Methodists, never given to enthusiasm, advertised revivals as "living water from Christ" and where descendants of Anglo-American settlers, an oral folk, nailed up hand-lettered signs:

WOOD F-
OR SALE

This Hill Country where Gipson lived is a haunting blend of convenience, part terrain, part vegetation, part culture. Its definition and boundaries have been variously interpreted. A transitional ecotone, it started as a human region with the convergence in the mid-nineteenth century of three diverse heritages—an enigma at the heart of an already enigmatic state. When these heritages coalesced in the twentieth century, something emerged that was vernacular and visionary, something of a fortress mentality of beating the odds, building a little world, keeping it going. From this heritage of people and place the region raised a writer and a president, who were born and who died within a few weeks and sixty miles of each other. An understanding of them, as biographers of Lyndon Johnson recognize, begins with their setting—an atavistic, and sometimes animistic crucible in a changing world. As the popular appeal of the ethos evoked by this setting waned or waxed, so too over the years has the Hill Country lessened or grown. When Gipson and Johnson were born there in 1908 the Hill Country included about sixteen counties west of Austin and west-northwest of San Antonio. Since their deaths in 1973 and the subsequent popularization of the area through the song "Luckenbach, Texas" by Waylon Jennings and Willie Nelson, outposts of "Hill Country living" have stretched east toward Houston and north toward Dallas–Fort Worth in a four-hundred-mile crescent in the center of the state.

Gipson's Hill Country is part of the Edwards Plateau, the southernmost extent of the Great Plains of North America. Subhumid, no longer forest and not yet desert, soils shallow and rocky, with sparse to moderate vegetation, plains grasses, deciduous tree cover, and some evergreens (about which ranchers would say "too many"), the eroded tableland is drained by small rivers, their flows varying with the erratic rainfalls. Culturally a mixture of Anglo-American and Hispanic cultures with a predominantly German cultural block, this scarpland, never able to support much of a population, punctuates the final part of the high plateau before the uplifted terrain gives way to the fertile, Texas blackland prairies and coastal plains.

The general undesirability of this area that Gipson learned to know as a boy protected its earliest historic inhabitants, the Tonkawas, from all but seasonal incursions of Comanches and Apaches. Spanish explorers passed briefly through the region. Their expeditions slowed in the eroded valleys and brushy toplands. They raised crosses to mark several hilltops. When they left, they never came back. The obstacles guarded no great treasures. Only the markers and the legends remained. European civilization stopped at the lower, eastern edge of the Balcones Escarpment where springs watered San Antonio de Béxar and San Marcos de Neve, until 1845, when Germans penetrated this wilderness.[1]

This little world had become an uneasy union of place and people and history by the time Fred Gipson was old enough to cross a rickety suspension bridge over an intermittent Comanche Creek in order to reach school in Mason each morning and to return home in the afternoon to his chores, then perhaps to slip away to fish or hunt or wander the hills. Through a boy's eyes it was a land of arrowheads, legends, and wildlife.[2] As he grew older, he saw it was a poor land, its people becoming increasingly poor because of their dependence upon rain and their unwise land-use practices. He heard his father threaten to shoot holes in the clouds to make them release their water.[3] He himself daydreamed that someday he would find something independent of the vagaries of weather to carry him to riches. For a boy seeking riches on earth and a man who distrusted faith, this declined, romantic horizon may have been unsettling. "He returned to it religiously again and again," his surviving son later said, "even though it probably wasn't the place he should have lived."[4] Yet the native landscape with its peculiar lighting and rich storytelling always inhabited Gipson's mind, and his life and writings show that he was never spared the "anguish of loving," as a later Texas novelist wrote of a similar character.[5]

His parents, Beck Gipson and Emma Deischler, labored, bought land, built a house, and aspired to be accepted into the social fabric of their little trilingual, almost tricultural, world. Forest folk descended from forest folk, Gipson's parents came from East Texas to Mason in 1899, carrying with them, according to a story told by Frank Wardlaw, an alligator egg which eventually hatched, "producing what was probably the first and only alligator ever born on the Llano."[6] From these beginnings, the family struggled to take root and to adapt. They considered themselves ordinary people, the father a bit dreamy-eyed and the mother the rock of the family, descended from "unbending hardshell, hard-bought" westerers and reared to active participation in making the society around them – such people as come later to populate Gipson's novels.[7]

Farm life was hard in Mason, but it was even harder for poor people like the Gipsons who subsisted from one rain to the next until they acquired land and surplus. When chores were done at night, people turned to storytelling, yeoman and sharecropper alike recounting a lore boisterous and episodic, one story connected to another by a strong, unspoken, didactic frame. Such formulaic narratives were told both for fun and profit, functioning as cheap entertainment and as social correctives. Like gossip, they titillated and admonished. The theme of luck recurred, along with reminders of the amount of work it took to make money. The stories advised slow and steady progress over chancy speculations. They were old tales abounding in epithets, the stock and trade of traditional societies. They preserved and transmitted cultural values, and they could substitute for social interaction, even as they were a medium for such interaction.[8]

From these narratives, and from his family's perspective on the outer social edge of the county, young Fred Gipson developed a sense of community. He heard in these stories the patterns and forms that later developed into a literary style: elliptical and anecdotal, with large narrative leaps and with insight into personality and events. Through such tales he acquired a way of dealing with people, seeing them through the filter of storytelling, as if they were part of a universal tale that had meaning to all people in all places and at all times. He came to prefer local people that way—as types, as a group, as photographs that could not disappoint.[9]

Gipson grew to adulthood in a community in which the home, the extended family, the livelihood of the people, and the landscape shaped life. Mason and the small network of farm villages in the rural county still constituted a traditional, or sacred, community, in contrast to many other parts of an already urbanizing and secularizing state. Social contacts were primary; tradition played a large part in individual life; personal obligations dominated even the economic sphere; there was a mutual effort to sustain self-sufficiency; the forces of gossip and tradition were powerful tools of social control; and the value system was impermeable.[10] In general, the families were patriarchal and people were age-oriented. Large families were favored, and children were given chores according to their ages and sex. Work retained a secondary social function, shared work affording a sense of community, and games of mimesis, pranks, and joking were highly developed. Farmsteads presented a picture of status, more so than house and clothing. For most of the people, the landscape was imbued with the qualities of early settlers who had named its features, and a rich oral tradition was sustained as much through geographic landmarks as it was through bricoleurs and raconteurs. Social differences among families were not always visible to the untrained eye and were considered largely hereditary, yet rare was the fifteen-year-old who lacked a pretty clear notion of his family's elaborately contrived rank.[11] For a boy like Fred Gipson, growing up in the 1910s and 1920s, life was picturesque and simple, though hard, and the land was the fixed point by which he knew his relationship to everyone and everything else.[12]

The New Deal dominated the turbulent political scene during Gipson's early adulthood, even though the region where Gipson grew to maturity was a Republican bastion in an otherwise

Democratic state. The Germans there still blamed Democrats for starting the Civil War, and officially they did not care for the New Deal. Like the Elect they considered themselves to be, they cultivated their virtues, saved, and almost as a bloc voted Republican.

Gipson's life is told again and again in his novels, from his birth in 1908 in a small farmhouse outside Mason, the first son in a family that already included four daughters, to his parents' construction of a frame dwelling (the earlier children having been born in a picket hut on a tract of land that was part of the old Ben Gooch place—named, as most of the land was named, after the early settler). Never very fertile, the land was almost worn out. Without rain, it baked and cracked. A boy doing his chores and working in the corn and cotton fields—chopping weeds or hauling rocks to the fence line—had ample time and room to daydream. Such a childhood schooled the imagination: the landscape, punctuated by rocks, brown and reddish gray for most of the year; in spring, grasses and weeds and bluebonnets and Indian blankets hastening to flower and seed before hundred-degree summers forced life inside and back underground. If rains came again in September, the crops would grow enough to weather the winter, feed the whitetail deer, and ripen to harvest the following spring. But rainfall and good luck would be hard to predict, and ventures succeeded or failed purely by quirks of weather and market, regardless of how much Anglo muscle, virtue, devotion, or selection went into their making.

Growing up with five mothers, so to speak, young Gipson had a short childhood in a home ruled by women. Members of the family said he was "born grown." Much younger than his four older sisters, he escaped by taking to the outdoors and climbing hills and scaling rock outcroppings. He never overcame this youthful pattern, his surviving son later affirmed; women came to represent a whole life toward which he became increasingly alienated, linking them with religion and its concept of sin.[13]

By the time Gipson followed his sisters across Comanche Creek to the grammar school in Mason, he had already become an explorer, a fisher, a dreamer, an apprentice storyteller to his father and other older raconteurs.[14] Getting rich quickly was his favorite daydream, and young Gipson often tried to make that dream come true. The family tells of a time when he captured a rattlesnake in order to sell its venom to a San Antonio pharmaceutical firm.[15] He never lost his early habit of looking for hidden values in the scarpland where he grew up. He loved the land, everyone who knew him would say; but the people who lived there he could not stand.[16]

Gipson learned early the joys of hunting and the stigma of poverty attached to the Anglo-American families north and east of Mason, the poor areas where the soil was thin and poor—or had become thin and poor through Anglo misuse, the Germans would murmur, and county agents would confirm. He became sensitive and defensive about his family's background, that they were poor and had been there so short a time compared to Germans who had come to the area in the 1840s and 1850s. As he became older, he brooded over the disadvantages and the prejudices he encountered. He learned to despise the comfort of faith. He hated carelessness and respected self-dignity. The erosion of the land became a symbol for him of the decline of people and community. "He missed somewhere the value and power of forgiveness," his son Beck recalled. "He wouldn't slough other people's thoughtless offenses off." Likewise, he would not forgive the land for eroding. "Even with his practice of soil conservation, he tried to reach back rather than forward." The older Gipson grew, the more he felt himself caught in a "time trap." He was "a full generation behind the country" in his outlook and "would have liked to have been a rancher to have seen what it was like then." He loved the land, not so much for what it was as for what it might once have been.

In high school Gipson found outlets for his intense introspection. He read incessantly. He helped order books for the school library. He wrote for the school annual, and his first published work was a short story for it entitled "Luck." He debated as a member of the Lone Star Club against members of the rival Woodrow Wilson Club, both organizations founded and sponsored by school superintendent S. N. Dobie.[17] When he graduated in 1926 as one of thirty-eight seniors, he stopped writing but he continued to read classics (his daughter-in-law remembered *Jane Eyre, Robinson Crusoe,* and *The Call of the Wild*), Zane Grey westerns, and Texana.

For seven years after he graduated, this landscape and its legends and lore grew in him until he followed his younger brother to the University of Texas in 1933 and resumed writing. In Austin the remembered native countryside recurs in essays, stories, and novels—different characters, different plots, same bonding of both character and plot to setting, always a kind of reverie:

> Our ramblings carried us into a broken region of granite upthrusts. Erosion had cut the huge masses of stone into a maze of labyrinthine passages, a network of shadowy caves. In that seclusion of this wild retreat I had once commanded a band of cutthroats who plundered all the neighboring villages and carried off fair maidens to hold for ransom.[18]

Sometimes in the early writings, Gipson's characters are overdrawn, too homespun or folksy to weather well, and sometimes the plots are too episodic, but his settings of land and sky and wind and weather are always sure. Settings hold the works together, convey meaning, and animate.

> They promise miles of tramping over rough, frosty terrain, through catclaw thickets that make tatters of frost-bitten ears and hands.

> Miles of struggling up boulder-strewn slopes, only to slip and fall down over the ledges on the other side of the hill. More more, through acres and acres of cacti that stick in your legs on one side so you'll jump and get stuck in the other.[19]

Land and weather are only rarely gentle or consistent, but they are omnipresent, coherent, and symbolic. However harsh and inconsistent this cradle of the soul was to Gipson during his childhood, it was a scene where the human presence loomed and lingered: a contradictory scene, realistic in detail and romantic in vision. Throughout his life Gipson liked to be photographed either against such backdrops or while fishing or hunting, as the family photograph collection shows.

These webs of place remembered—the place phantom—became the stuff of life and memory that Gipson would weave into literature: voices, heat ghosts, that haunt the farmsteads, inhabit the burial grounds, and speak in the stifling shade of oak clumps; the stories attached to bends in roads; the spirits of the early ones who named the places and who lived on in episodes that connected the trees, hills, and fields. The integration of such impressions—the "bits and pieces of folklore," as Sam Henderson wrote—into myth became a special richness of Gipson's writing. It was traditional, and also transcended traditions in what became a kind of argumentative posture.[20] Even if his books grew from the thin soil of the Hill Country, they were sustained by powerful and persistent taproots. For better or worse, these books would remain vernacular and visionary: as resonant in their setting as nineteenth-century folk architecture attuned itself to environment in ways that are always being rediscovered in a family of *New Shelter* magazines that tell the back-to-basics great-grandchildren what their grandparents still remembered. Gipson's writings would be quiet and almost fatalistic. They would teach waiting and simplification. Without supporting the organized religions that he strenuously opposed—that had "spooked him" already when he was young, his heirs would say—these writings would speak with the voice of medieval peasantry to their God: Save us from the king, save us from the bishop, save us from everything outside our parish and let us tend our own fields and herds. Teach us that often progress means holding your own, not losing ground.

CHAPTER TWO

"One Step Further" *1933–1937*

Fred Gipson's life became a search for good luck after he left Comanche Creek in 1933. His father had never been able to "shoot the clouds" to make them rain, and so far all of Gipson's own plans to get rich had failed. Twenty-five years old and not yet settled, frustrated by dim prospects at home, his parents still poor, Gipson followed his younger brother to the university in order to find some other, more promising route to success. With his neighbors and brothers-in-law, he joked about the plans he had if he could secure wealth. Mainly, he said, he wanted to become "aristocratic," at least for as long as he could, he added, knowing from his childhood on a dry-land farm that luck was the principal arbiter between success and failure and that good luck could depart as suddenly as it came.

Gipson also knew that a person down on his luck had no fear of losing the favor of fortune and could be happy—playing hooky, stealing watermelons, working fourteen hours a day on the road crew and happy for the overtime. Only after luck took a turn for the better did worry develop about fortune continuing. Though good luck and happiness should go together, they seldom did.

In Austin he first undertook through his writings to interpret his past—partly to explain himself to others, partly to sell work and pass courses, partly to sound his own depths and practice the craft. Nearly forty *Daily Texan* sketches, tales, and features focus autobiographically on Gipson (or a person like him) caught between country and city.[1] Sometimes they show university life through a country boy's eyes: the innocent and the city girl, the football team as a herd of steers. Sometimes they show a slice of cowboy life to campus readers: two ranch hands go to a border town, bulldog a sow, and lose all their money in the Rio Grande. Always these writings show manners and values of the urban and rural communities in confrontation.[2] They show that however much Gipson wanted the material successes that lay beyond Mason, Austin invited a break with a past which he invested with meaning and precedent. He became increasingly possessive of that past but felt at home neither with it nor in the city, as his many later moves would confirm.

In these writings, Gipson manifested a pronounced tendency to cling to, even to exaggerate, dialect.[3] The writings invariably lead back to the land and to the scenes of childhood that exerted an ever stronger pull on Gipson the older he became. Above everything else, however, the writings show the author remembering the land in the face of change, division, and ambivalence. Critics might later comment on deficiencies of plot or characterization in Gipson's writing, but never of setting.[4] Eventually the land became not only an orientation to thinking but also a way of thinking—a kind of "visual thinking" that helped him order memory and pattern experience.[5]

Moving back and forth between the two worlds was hard, Gipson explained. Austin and Comanche Creek differed in work and sleep, in speech and behavior, and in words and objectives. Some conflicts were serious, others mundane, as for example getting back to Mason late and having to work livestock the next morning.

> I went to bed the other night at the regular university-student bedtime and had just dropped off for a couple of minutes or so, when the old box telephone in the hall cut loose. I jumped and grabbed the receiver and shouted "hello!" and rattled the hook a few times. You always shout at party-line telephones and rattle their hooks. It's a sort of country ritual or something. Everybody does it.
>
> A thunderous "hello" came out of the receiver. Then I had to wait a little while the other party performed corresponding antics with his receiver-hook before I found out that it was the brother-in-law and he wanted help to round up some sheep.
>
> "All right," I shouted. "When do you want me to come?"
>
> "Right now," he shouted.
>
> I shouted again: "But, I've just gone to bed."
>
> He shouted again: "No, you're just getting up."
>
> I rattled the receiver-hook and slapped the box a slap or two, so I could get time to figure it all out. Then I said:
>
> "But, it's mighty early to hunt sheep now; and, anyway, I was a cattleman before I went to school and I'm still a cattleman at heart, and cattlemen and sheepmen don't get along. Read your books."
>
> I heard him rattle the hook, then, and I think maybe he kicked the wall.
>
> "I," he began, "don't care what you were before you went to school. I don't care what you are now. . . . I need help, and it looks like you'd at least appreciate all the money I've loaned you enough to help me out in a jam—even if you won't pay it back."[6]

The stories show Gipson's understanding of setting as context for characterization and action, his appreciation for formulaic behavior, and his schooling in the oral heritage. But as later life would show, his folk expression often masked problems that he never resolved successfully. Had the extremes between his two worlds been even greater, as were Katherine Anne Porter's when she said that she wanted to live either in a world capital or the howling wilderness, he might, surprisingly, have made the transition more easily.

Fred Gipson was an adult when he entered the university in 1933 to learn journalism. Here he met historian Walter Prescott Webb and folklorist J. Frank Dobie, the first cousin of the superintendent of schools in Mason. The friendship with Webb grew close; the acquaintance with Dobie remained rough. With his classmates Gipson was popular because he was rambunctious and told entertaining stories. Few saw his withdrawn side and his depressions. In his last semesters at the university—he left in 1937, soon after his father's death in late 1936—he published a story in the *Southwest Review*, was elected president of the national journalism society chapter, and campaigned against censorship of the *Daily Texan*, where he also published weekly columns on subjects ranging from Mason County to aesthetics and the Spanish civil war.[7]

The friendships he formed at the university were lasting—and some of the last new friendships of his life—but there seemed in all of them an element of disparity. With his teachers, Gipson was somewhat anomalous: a student almost as old as some of his teachers and who occasionally took the academic regimen entirely too casually. "If I ever get around to it and it's not too much trouble, I'm going to start a movement against final exams," he wrote in 1936, after daydreaming through a final for which he managed to write "three paragraphs that were really original."

> I got to thinking . . . that on a bright sunshiny day . . . a man could lie on the flat of his back under a tree and, by locating a little opening in the branches to look through and looking mighty close, he could maybe see a star. It would be pretty pale and white-looking, but he could probably see it, all right. I'll bet there's lots of astronomy profs that never saw a star in the daytime through a treetop.

"But then," he admitted, turning back to his test, "lying on your back under the tree isn't a very good way to get to be a prof of any kind" (p. 78). With his classmates, he became a sort of father figure, a spokesman and a leader, his face already lined. And because Gipson devoted most of his free time to writing stories that would sell or get him through classes, his intermittent courtships made little progress.

Yet apart from luck and change, the subject of women dominated young Gipson's university writings. Dating and gift giving, for example, were expensive, and Gipson had to work hard and write page after page of stories to earn enough to keep girls attentive. "On Account of a Girl, Maybe" opens with a young man in "a sad predicament, . . . and such a promising young writer, too. . . . Search as he may, he can find nothing to write about" since his "lady grew indifferent" (p. 39). The yarns of his dating problems are replete with local color and pathos, but sometimes the intended humor seems portentous in light of Gipson's later life, as when he warns, comparing women to beasts of burden in "That Sloe-Eyed Gal of the Blackjacks," that

> The main trouble with a heap of women (said Duke McKay—though the topic of conversation had been horses all afternoon) is thet you jist can't never figger 'em out, ner put no confidence in 'em. Doggone their hides, looks like they don't never even know theirselves one minute what they're liable to do the next. (P. 141)

For a man's own good, Gipson continues, a woman needed to be "gentled" and eased into hobbles, "no matter how she's been a-actin' toward you." Then he concludes, shifting the subject, "She ain't a-gonna run true to form, and you can jist figger on thet" (p. 147).

Women were often thus associated in these university writings with time and fortune, and from both time and fortune Gipson feared betrayal. Frequently linked with metaphors of the hunt, autumn, and sunset, women represent the end of freedom, the coming and going of the seasons, renewal predicated on death. These deep structures of the picturing mind are startling in direction and point to problems of estrangement waiting to occur.

> I like to watch leaves fall.
>
> I like to watch them whirl in the wind and skitter across pavements, drop in water and sail off, clutter up lawns.
>
> But most of all, I like them to fill up ditches.
>
> The reason I like them to fill up ditches is because then you can wade in them like you used to do when you were a kid.
>
> Of course, you can't wade in them much, now that you are grown. . . . People will think you foolish if they catch you walking along in a leaf-filled ditch. They can't understand how anybody could get enjoyment out of wading in dry leaves.
>
> They don't know how that dragging rustle and crackling of leaves under your feet makes you think back to clear starlit nights when you and another ragged, dirty-nosed kid trampled miles through the woods to the tune of a bell-mouthed potlikker hound whose one purpose in life was to tree 'possums. They don't know that.
>
> And if they knew that along with the memories of 'possum hunts, the rustle of leaves underfoot made you think of the swish of satin evening gowns, of the sparkle and glamour and gaiety of ballrooms, of soft eyes in shadowed corners—if they knew all of that, they'd howl with the incongruity of it.
>
> 'Possum hunts and lovely women—they don't fit into the same pattern. Not to other people, they don't. (Pp. 121–22)

Gipson's world, childlike in wonder and suggesting a writer who would choose to be detained in childhood, is also clear, dry, and solitary—starlit, night or day. He seems to have wanted to pursue and capture things clean and whole, every hunt a pursuit of the Big Adventure.

Gipson's images are probably no more crisscrossed than those of many young men part way between twenty and thirty, but in a storymaker who trafficks in scenes of the mind and who is subject to becoming the stories he tells, troubling currents are evident that could eventually erode his mindscape. It cannot be viewed as coincidence that he would eventually strike out at his own wife as his central symbol for the passage of time—for aging—in the same way that he struck literally at the people and forces that polluted Mason County's air and ruined its landscape, which he liked to see from "a high place somewhere in the early mornings where you can sit and watch a rising sun dig into a mist-filled valley below . . ." (p. 121).

Ever again in these nearly forty short pieces, when he is alone he is somewhere up high, it is early, and he happily watches the beginnings: of day as in sunrise and fog lifting, of initiation as in the hunt, of self making a fresh start.

Some of Gipson's student work records rituals of rural folk life. His popular column "One Thing and Then Another" frequently included such passages, but his finest story published in the university newspaper was a reflexive tale entitled "Sweet Potatoes," written in 1935. A frame story of a storyteller telling about a storyteller, this piece shows two of Gipson's most memorable characters from his early writing. Duke McKay is an itinerant trader, assisted by Smoky, who occasionally steals back what has been sold before, or who steals what can soon be sold elsewhere. Dealing in hot goods keeps these two—McKay plays the straight man to Smoky's villainy—"traveling light" through East Texas until a theft of some sweet potatoes finds them looking up the barrel of a six-foot shotgun held by a cross-eyed old man they called Grey-Whiskers. The story then speeds toward a double-twist surprise ending.

> Here Duke stopped and sat grinning into the fire. I waited; but evidently he was through. Finally I asked: "What about Smoky? Did the scare cure him of stealing?"

> Duke rolled a stingy little cigarette and lit it. "Who, that black rascal? You know what! When I finished down there and got back to Jacksonville, I happened to unroll a old tarp what I hadn't been a-usin' none; and what do you think was in it? Well I'll tell you. It was thet old shot-gun! It's up at old man Weaver's now. Make me think of it, and I'll show it to you some time!" (P. 28)

A formula story, to be sure, but one in which Gipson masterfully recorded the oral performance rituals of folktales with an accuracy that comes of close listening.

The university stories are especially happy when Gipson recalls the rituals of his childhood—what Robert Marett has called simple folk sacraments that attach to eating, fighting, mating, educating, governing, judging, covenanting, healing, and dying.[8] Even Gipson's dog stories are ritualized, from dogs registering for classes at the university to dogs practicing rituals of the chase passed down, one dog to the next, for generations. A dog, Gipson asserted, could be "very conscientious" about rituals. "And lots of times, after he's already gone a good ways ahead, he gets to thinking maybe he hasn't done it just right, and comes back to do it all over again" (p. 46). Raccoons and other varmints could also behave ritualistically. Such rituals of the quarry gave "a man a chance to keep up without any trouble" and to referee the sport of the kill. "Yes, a man who knows how to go about it can have some might good sport at 'coon-hunting, without straining himself at all" (p. 48).

With equal finesse Gipson described the advent of a weather change or the visit of someone like "Hard Pressed Sam," the tick inspector who rushed in to visit the narrator's parents—dreamy-eyed father named Beck and rock of a mother—just long enough to fill himself with four or five substantial meals before rushing on to the next dry-land farm. The really admirable thing about Sam, whose visits made the father's eyes twinkle (p. 53) and gave the mother a "look of resentment" (p. 52), was that Sam was a

"Fellow Who Didn't Have No Time" (p. 49). Revealing too because it shows the young son of the family as an only child, the story places the son in a crossfire of parental and vocational values. As with the oral transmission stories like "Sweet Potatoes," Gipson is always the sole object of attention, the inheritor and interpreter of the old to the new.

When he was not imagining himself returned to boyhood or as the commander of a band of cutthroats "who plundered all the neighboring villages and carried off fair maidens to hold for ransom" (p. 107), Gipson wrote of himself crusading "toward the final Utopia" (p. 120), rich beyond dreams from having cached so many hides at so many dollars apiece—always some way "to experience the exotic feeling of irresponsibleness associated with that age when a lifetime can be lived in a day and a year is measured by the eternity of time from one Christmas to another" (p. 104). Often in these pastoral moments he exaggerated himself as a country rustic, his stories frequently undercut by some line or act that permits the teller to step aside if the story comes under attack: "There's no point to this story. So don't read it and sit back and shake your head. . . . I just mean to write a story about me and some other people . . ." (p. 122). The important thing about these stories, he suggested in a column in 1936, was to write enough stories to "get rich and become aristocratic" (p. 89).

Gipson's picture world was already formed when he went to Austin. Much of what he learned after he left Mason was assimilated but not appropriated. In his worst moments, Gipson saw Austin competing with the world of Comanche Creek; in his better moods, he became a carrier of two worlds. Gipson's symbology derived from his homemade world. What metaphors he had for self and society reposed in that mythic landscape, and any adjustments between the sacred and secular, private and public spheres could be accommodated only at the expense of his interior world. As he would react in later years to the physical erosion of his Mason County landscape, so he reacted with violence—still submerged—and feelings of betrayal, to any loss sustained to his mindscape. This rhetoric of loss pervades his writings, and turns ultimately into a kind of efficient, self-fulfilling ethos.

Despite the bravado of his university writings for the *Daily Texan*, Gipson's early journalism reveals a stridence that belies the backwoods, upstream, folksy wisdom the columns are intended to communicate. Part of that is the problem of a young writer finding a voice. But part also is Gipson's reversion in Austin to something that he had opposed before: the kind of drugstore backwoodsiness used to prove something.[9] Ultimately a peculiar but persistent kind of double vision would always trouble Gipson. A son of the Hill Country ethos, he tended to let his eye drift from a realistic foreground to a romanticized and visionary horizon. Thus the tension in moving between Mason and Austin. Thus his pattern of liking from afar what he had detested up close, and would detest again when he succeeded in getting it back. Thus too his propensity, especially as he grew older, to hate individuals while telling their stories with compassion. The pattern recurred in Gipson's attitudes toward time, places, and people. Already as a student he pictured himself regretting the lost moment, and he set out in search for what might have been.

He wrote intensely of the rites of passage and celebrations of everyday life that in Austin troubled him most. He drew freely on his boyhood recollections, and if he did not yet sense a divergence, his writings nonetheless show a splitting of the self: between romanticism and realism, between what he wished and what he knew would be, between what he saw and what he thought he remembered, between wanting to recover lost time and catch up with his age group—and not really wanting to grow up at all. On more than one occasion he compared the rituals and formulas of rural folk with metaphors that suggest an almost catastrophic vision of violent encounter between reality and memory—in which living, not only living in the country, but all living, becomes time's victim.

He wrote both longingly and revealingly of a "poor baffled writer . . . who will spring out of his bed some morning, his head whirling. . . . To the typewriter he will dash and, in a few minutes, slap out a piece of work that will startle the world. Then he will become famous and grow a dinky little mustache for the women to admire and microbes to inhabit. . . . And people will be proud to say that they know a man who has advanced the world one step further towards the final Utopia" (p. 41).

In a universe where advance was triggered by fortune, Gipson's world was a mythological extension of the natural world where wolves once reigned supreme, all the other animals quaking when the wolf's call pierced the night (pp. 44–45). Though wolves only occasionally marauded the Hill Country, the memory of the wild dog is a potent theme in Gipson's writing because it reveals forces internalized and then domesticated. With Gipson's natural symbols—and tales can be symbols—the emphasis must be placed on symbol as well as on nature, on the purpose and connectedness of the tale as well as on the story as story. Gipson's fatalistic peasant ethos survived, less generative perhaps than before but still capable of change even if pointed toward closure.[10] Eventually, as Gipson shows in using the word *further* in routing his way toward Utopia, the quest would become a journey into a state of mind.

CHAPTER THREE

"Gifts of God That Were Free to All," 1944–1949

My Grandma Elfie Creech used to have a saying. She said that generally in everyone's life there is a time when he is more himself than at any other time between birth and death.

Opening of RECOLLECTION CREEK

Whether Fred Gipson experienced such a time of "being more himself" or was conscious of it if in fact it occurred, nothing better informs his work than does this outlook—nor burned more steadily than his quest to recapture the fortunate moment.

Gipson's three most original works—*Recollection Creek* (1944–48, 1955), *Fabulous Empire* (1946), and *Hound-Dog Man* (1949)—have been slighted in favor of *Old Yeller* and other juveniles. But these first three major works open the window to Gipson's soul. In them converge the many poetically autobiographical themes and issues that remained with Gipson throughout his writing. They introduce the "whole repertory company," so to speak, using Gore Vidal's words, with which Gipson grew up.[1] They present his landscape as serene, sunlit, radiant—almost with one voice attesting to his need for space and solitude.

Recollection Creek, as much a place book as it is a people book, reveals scenes of the mind that lingered nostalgically in Gipson's later novels as a yearning after the Golden Age. Several loosely connected short stories that were first published between 1944 and 1948 were gathered and reworked into the novel of 1955, *Recollection Creek*, which represents Gipson's first major narrative expression. While Gipson worked on this novel and kept his family fed by publishing the individual stories, he was also in these years writing two other books in which he tried to resolve the troubling implications of the opening vignette.

Because Gipson's openings are especially revealing as critical commentaries, showing more about a novel than he may show anywhere else, and because this novel richly informs Gipson's other works, giving an episodic career coherence and pattern, the opening warrants explication with an eye to what Leon Edel suggests when he writes that criticism is "partially a biographical process."[2]

Recollection Creek is a frame narrative. Like an afternoon's reverie culminating in a stream of associations, the novel is a retrospection of youth and innocence and happiness. The setting resembles the geography and climate of the Hill Country. The time is around the turn of the century. The narrator is older now, maybe much older, and alone when this daydream starts, and his memories are unguarded as he focuses his eyes on "that rare period of living when the days are especially bright, the world is extra new, and the events that transpire are so full of color, excitement, and high drama that, forever afterward, that time is a shiny little gem of remembrance, holding for the one who owns it a special, though often mysterious, significance."[3]

The frame gradually turns into story pure and simple: a boy and a dog, a cousin and a whole extended family, and no school for a term because there had been "a killing over a trustee election" and "somebody burned the Squaw Springs schoolhouse to the ground" (pp. 1–2). The two boys were free to run wild, to become natural savages, and to learn the essence of everything—the insight into honor, manliness, duty, or whatever the rest of their lives would turn on. However much experience might have been lacking in the setting of Recollection Creek, a ready way of encountering life allegorically gave each person there a spiritual kinship with a past invested with meaning and precedent. Being free, the boys can discover the bonds that hold their community together. Observers at the beginning, they become participants in folk ritual before the novel ends. These things the narrator remembers during the several hours while Recollection Creek flowed again.

Hopper Creech, the narrator, is nine when the frame appears. His cousin Jay is a "freckle-nosed ten . . . so full of that restless, reckless spirit that grownups like to call 'pure devilment' that just having him around seemed to give an added charge of excitement to every event" (p. 2). Just before the narrative gets under way, Hopper muses to himself, "it could be that Jay had more to do with bringing my life into sharp focus during that short period than I ever realized" (p. 2).

The narrator gradually acquires character, while his Grandma Elfie Creech has strong character from the opening paragraph. Her name speaks generations of westering: upper South stock, fundamentalistic, backbone of family and community. Years later, after this and subsequent novels made Gipson famous, he fictionalized his family history and gave himself grandparents and background where he had never had them. His grandparents, he said, had settled on the San Saba, making him the third generation of his family in the Hill Country. In truth, Fred Gipson never knew his grandparents, and his family was turn-of-the-century new in Mason County. The importance to Gipson of extended family and his own desire to have roots, like the German families in the better parts of the county, are thus recalled in the novel's opening words.

As the focus narrows and the frame drops from view, the narrative wraps itself around a central motif in relation to which the other images and themes in a tightly constructed fiction derive their relative values, a device Gipson likely fashioned through astute observation of oral performance—much as he learned to suggest in his writing the pauses by which all speakers create effects, heighten tension, leave the understood unsaid, or invent a way to go on. The emblem of this motif is a solitary silhouette named Aaron Blood, the memory of whom brings Hopper and his cousin Jay into the story proper. The most haunting and enigmatic character in all Gipson's fiction, Aaron Blood is an awkward recluse who disdains to speak to adults, preferring to share only with children whatever ties still connect him with humanity. When adults crowd him, however, Aaron Blood can speak to them with a kind of backward eloquence, showing him to be more than they suspect and more too than they are. A misanthrope who nonetheless loves people he deems worthy of love, Blood proves generous and fair as he rides about the countryside on "a big roan bull."

> Blood was a queer sort of man. Not that he looked especially queer, other than when he rode the bull. He was about medium height, a little on the stout side, black-headed, blue-eyed, and slow of movement. He wore the blue overalls and block-toed shoes that dry-land farmers generally wore. He wore the same broad-brimmed, high crowned hat that was common in those days.
>
> But the way he wore that hat set him apart a little. You never saw a crease or dent in it. You never saw it marred by a speck of dust or a streak of grease or sweat. When he put it on, he took as much time and pains as a woman to set it exactly as he wanted it, and the way he wanted it was sitting straight and stiff on his head, so low down that its weight generally bent his ears a little. (P. 3)

Through the recollection of the hat worn as only the most deliberate outcast would wear it, Gipson's Hopper, now young, recalls Blood's attitude toward other grown folks.

> I think he hated them. I know he had no more dealings with them than was absolutely necessary. When circumstances forced him to exchange words with other men, he seemed to resent it. He'd speak, all right, but in a vicious, sharp tone calculated to end the conversation as quickly as possible.

"But with me—and with Jay, after Jay came, Blood was different" (p. 4), Hopper remembers. He remembers a time when Jay incited Aaron Blood to race his bull in a horse race that charged three dollars' admission "For Anything that Wears Hair and Runs on Four Feet" (p. 6). Recalling an episode from Gipson's youth when he was almost trampled by a stampeding steer during a mock buffalo-killing performance by Herman Lehmann, for many years a Comanche captive,[4] the tale of Aaron Blood's jackpot is a masterpiece of telescoped action and fictional craft and one of the funniest and happiest passages in some three thousand printed pages of Gipson's writing.

A picaresque fantasy with strong pastoral and elegiac elements, *Recollection Creek* is a Texas *Huck Finn.* With Blood as their occasional guide, Hopper and Jay Creech embark on their year of being more themselves than at any other time before or since. The boys, witnesses to the hunting escapades of their supposedly wiser elders, themselves learn to hunt. They witness proverbial conflicts between the sexes, but apart from their annoyances with girls, the boys are separated from these conflicts until near the end of the novel.[5] They learn lore and the structure of stories. They plan to get rich with the help of old Restless Solomon, who swears to the boys' parents that his "'drifting days is done'" if they will only give him and his bent wife a chance to get on their feet. "'A man's got to light and stick if he ever aims to amount to anything in this world. . . . That's the only way'" (p. 38). "'I always liked Restless,' Jay admits."

> I believed in him. He'd talk to a boy like he would to a grown man. He kept good hunting dogs and he had a lot of good hunting yarns

> to tell. And around the fire at night, he'd play his mouth harp so pretty it made the tears come, and I'd have to hold back hard to keep from crying out loud. (P. 40)

Restless taught them, "'Yonder's the woods full of good easy money, running loose . . .'" (p. 41). But after they walk some seven or more miles, following a tiny 'possum that could "'run like a Mexican lion'" (p. 90), the boys and Restless take up quail hatching (a half million dollars' sure profit) and eventually even cat and 'possum fighting, convinced always that "great wealth" was right at their fingertips (p. 131). But the fighting cat overturns a lantern that ignites the hay in the barn where the quail fledglings are about to create a 1,500 percent profit, and the boys watch barn and house burn, becoming impoverished but wiser. Restless Solomon sells out to the neighbors for a little more than he owed them—thereby securing the only substantial profit anywhere in the novel apart from one young buck's winning a bride in Jay's older sister—and the boys see a glimmer of truth when the men of Recollection Creek meet to bail out Restless and his wife. "'We'll hit the road again and try to make out somehow,'" Restless tells them morosely.

> "Ain't no use in hanging on when you know you're done beat. Don't reckon it was meant for me and mine to have nothing, like other folks."
>
> He sucked in another deep, shuddering breath and let it out. "But it's pure hard," he added in a pitiful voice, "having to drive off and leave my crop. Prettiest prospects in the country! . . . Ain't hardly no amount of money can pay for it." (Pp. 150–51)

The boys witness their fathers and uncles buying the overpriced crop, and then Hopper continues:

> As was the custom in those days when somebody had a burnout, the neighbors all pitched in and loaded Restless's wagon with sacks of corn, bed quilts, bacon, furniture, and clothes till, accord-

> ing to Papa, Restless left Recollection Creek with a wagon piled twice as high as it had been when he came.
>
> Restless accepted the gifts with dignity and solemn thanks.
>
> Just before he started to drive away, he came to where Jay and I stood leaning against a tree, trying to keep as far away from our papas as we could get. . . .
>
> "How'd the fight come out?" he whispered.
>
> "All right, I guess," I said nervously.
>
> After setting fire to Restless's house and burning him out, I felt so guilty that I couldn't meet his eyes.
>
> "Knowed it would," he whispered. "Knowed it all the time. . . ."
>
> I looked up, surprised. Restless's voice didn't sound at all like that of a man who'd just suffered a burn-out. It was just as eager and excited as ever.
>
> "Man, oh man! I wish I could have been there to have seen the scrap!" he said.
>
> For a second there, I could have sworn Restless was ready to break out with a big laugh.
>
> But just then Papa walked up and I saw that I'd been wrong. Because, as quick as Restless noticed Papa, his face got sober again. And it stayed that way as he turned and walked back toward the loaded wagon. And he walked slow and tired-like, with his shoulders slumped and his feet dragging the ground. Just the way you'd expect a man to walk when hard luck's robbed him of everything he owns and he's forced to go on the drift again. (Pp. 151–53)

In the voice of the boy but recalled as a man, Hopper concludes ironically, "Even yet, I get an uncomfortable feeling when I think of how Jay and I brought ruin to our friend Restless Solomon" (p. 153). In this episode Hopper learns about people, and he employs conventions to mask his new awareness.

Told with insight, pauses, deliberation, and gesture, *Recollection Creek* flows from one remembered scene to another, babbling, running wide or deep, as streams will do. Linking the stories in one way are episodes with the boys' grandparents, culminating in old Grandpa Vesper Creech's fatal encounter with a phantom turkey. Linking the stories in another way are numerous occasions when the boys witness, and occasionally try to foil, rites of passage. They throw rocks to shy the horse that Jay's sister's horsebreaking suitor rides, dropping the proud Ruel MacLaurin—"Sometimes when he came riding in off the range, he glittered and blazed in the sunlight like a big jewel" (p. 31)—right into the middle of a prickly-pear clump. They learn how to bury chopped-off toes, and they bury their grandfather. They learn how to test dogs, and they learn how to test true love, or what passes for it among eighteen-year-olds in the community. "I wondered," Hopper says, "what there was about a man with a coon hound big enough to pack off a whole hog ham that made him better for marrying than his twin brother who owned an egg-sucking pup" (p. 67). They go to town and learn "city ways." They witness the ebb and flow of luck and learn "'Nobody ever made a fortune out of work'" (p. 79). They learn to talk like their fathers in the stock epithets of Recollection Creek.

Despite much that shows Gipson living in the lives of these boy characters, Gipson's ethos seems also embodied in the rigid, solitary figure of Aaron Blood, "riding his roan bull and wearing his black hat low over his bent ears" (p. 53). With Aaron Blood's help, the boys inflict the community's vengeance on selfish old man Tate Ishum, who goads the boys each year into stealing his melons, always the biggest and sweetest: "Sure, we'd swiped watermelons out of the old skinflint's patch. Plenty of times. But that wasn't stealing. Back in those days, nobody along Recollection Creek would have called it *stealing*" (pp. 157–58). Hopper explains, however, that "Folks just sort of lumped watermelons in the same category with water and air. . . ." He insists that they are "gifts of God that were free to all" (p. 158).

An outsider, Aaron Blood helps restore bonds that hold the community together not only with old Ishum but also with the

Creech fathers, when Blood gives Hopper and Jay two horses with saddles. "'I figured the black one for Jay and the bay for you,'" he tells Hopper. "Jay came suddenly to his feet. He said in astonishment: 'You mean, Mr. Blood, that you aim to give us them horses? Just flat-out *give* them to us'" (p. 202). Hopper, the adult, breaks into his reverie and says, "The best I recollect, we never did actually get around to thanking Aaron Blood. Boys our age generally don't have the right words to thank gods for their gifts" (p. 203). The fathers question Blood's motives and Hopper's father, Emil, rides with Hopper over to Aaron Blood's two-room shack (p. 205). "'You can't afford to go around giving away good horses and saddles to boys. What's on your mind? What are you after?'" (p. 205). Aaron Blood answers:

> "Well, Emil Creech . . . let me tell you something. I can afford to do whatever I goddam please with my money. I give them horses to them boys because I like 'em. I like 'em because they treat me like I was somebody and don't ask no questions. . . .
>
> "On top of that, I was a youngun once and I done some hoping and dreaming, just like them boys. You was a boy once and you done the same thing. And now look at us. Me, a crabby old fool, too soured out with life for the good Lord hisself to get along with. You, greedy as a hog and trying to git your hands on every piece of land in the country. So damned greedy and suspicious you can't let a man give your boy a present without looking for some meanness behind it." (P. 206)

Hopper is "glad it was dark" so nobody can see his burning shame (p. 205), but years pass before he understands what Aaron Blood meant.

> I'm pretty certain he was trying to say the same thing that Grandma Elfie meant by her saying—that, generally, there is a period in everyone's life when he is more himself than at any other time between birth and death.

> Only I don't think he'd been as lucky as Jay and I. I don't think that ever in his life Aaron Blood had known that wild, free, and irresponsible time when he actually felt really and truly *himself.* (P. 208)

One wonders about the relationship between Gipson, always on the lookout for something shiny, and Aaron Blood's misfortune which recurs in other Gipson characters, as does the theme of the fortunate moment when "gifts of God" like water and air and happiness "were free to all" and untainted.[6]

Parts of *Recollection Creek* are as moving as any settings and character sketches in Texas literature, but what makes the novel a watershed is that its prolonged composition frames the most significant years of Gipson's literary career. Any novel built from treasured and reused stories tends to be particularly revealing of an author's personal credo. Though combining of stories is highly characteristic of formulaic composition, *Recollection Creek* also expresses the state of Gipson's soul through the novel's elaborate analogies of landscape and folk memory. The medium of transmission of folk, or group, values is the act of storytelling, "subject to evaluation," as Richard Bauman has written, "both as truth and as art for the skill and effectiveness with which it is told."[7] *Recollection Creek* indexes a wide range of folk, etiological, and animal tales that rest in the mind long after one has left the novel: subversive scenes reflecting a way of life hardly viable but making some striking claims for preserving a deteriorating status quo. Though gentled by youth and obscured by convention, these scenes are at once radical and reactionary—radical in their presentation of the desire to break away entirely, reactionary in their presentation of the desire to turn time back or to return; radical *and* reactionary in their presentation of the desire to start over.

Gipson's life at this time also reflected the radical and reactionary, both muted by a Hill Country setting. After leaving the university, he had taken a job as a roving reporter in Corpus Christi, married, traveled to Mexico, and gotten fired. With his young wife expecting their first child, Gipson returned to Mason to build a small house on fifteen acres of land deeded to him by his widowed mother and to start building that curious outlook on life similar to what John Graves has since termed "backward progress."[8] The transition from the thirties to the forties had been punctuated by the start of World War II, Gipson narrowly missing induction after he and his wife moved to the Hill Country, and by a conservative mood of national consensus characteristic of war years. Gipson himself ricocheted between Austin and Mason during these years of intense apprenticeship. With the assistance of a university friend, Joe Small of Austin, Gipson succeeded in placing stories with *Collier's*, *Southwest Review*, and *Reader's Digest*, but a number of stories were returned with the criticism that the plots were too thin. Some later stories found their way into *Recollection Creek*. The story that made his fortune was "My Kind of Man," which appeared in 1944 in *Southwest Review*. With its publication, Gipson was commissioned by Donald Day to write a biography of Col. Zack Miller, famous as one of the colorful owners of the 101 Ranch Wild West Show of Ponca City, Oklahoma. This biography, *Fabulous Empire* (1946), was Gipson's first bestseller and is crucial in his career. The biography succeeds admirably. It is written with understanding, and it contains some of Gipson's most polished phrasing, the style closely attuned to the substance. Gipson employs fictional techniques to tell the story of Zack Miller, the aura of the heroic tale and the continental scope of a national epic informing the biography. In Gipson's hands, Miller's story becomes that of a man as well as of a land, and Gipson makes here explicit some of the feelings suggested in *Recollection Creek*.

Fabulous Empire seems almost as much about Gipson as about

Miller, with the author participating in the national myth as fully as his subject does. In the end, Zack Miller's life turns out to be what Fred Gipson's was to become. The symbolic portrait starts with melting pot and virgin land metaphors as Ponca Indians, the westering Miller family, and an Irish immigrant named Jimmy Moore (surrogate bachelor father of young Zack) converge on the Cherokee Strip of Oklahoma Territory. Ever his best in presenting setting, Gipson shows the raw empire just at its most fabulous, just as white settlers see it for the first time, before the grazing and plowing.

> The Strip was a cowman's paradise. Fifty-eight miles wide, a hundred and eighty long, it was one of the richest grasslands on the North American continent. It was a land of high, rolling prairies, wide valleys, and sweet living water. Timber grew along the watercourses, wild grape hung in the trees; there were tall pecans, elms, and thickets of wild plum. There were deer and turkey in the bottomlands where the bluestem grass grew tall as a horse. Out in the open were prairie chickens, and antelope grazed by the thousands upon buffalo grass so thick a man could pitch his hat out in any direction and it'd never touch the ground.[9]

Thus open the 1880s and 1890s on this landscape where Zack Miller's father held grazing rights to sixty thousand acres and where the 101 Ranch started. The world is colorful with Indian ceremonials, cattle drives, horse trading, profiteering, gunfights, grass wars. Here animals are named after foreign heads of state; the marks of mankind's progress are dwarfed by awesome expanses, and men were men and women were rare. Zack sets about learning all he can from the Ponca chief, Comesy; from his father; and from the Irish crew boss, Jimmy Moore. They teach him things that they alone know. Even as a boy, Zack realizes that such knowledge—like the "big yellow mastiff dog" (p. 125) that once saves him from death—is his greatest resource in encouraging fortune to come his way. He stores this knowledge and uses it with reserve, realizing that left alone, time is no ally. As he watches one after another of his mentors swept away, leaving him what they can, he begins to suspect the inevitability of bad luck and concludes that victory is holding one's own.

Gipson shows Zack Miller withstanding trial after trial, wounded yet not retreating, but one loss cuts deeply, and Gipson too would someday feel such loss. In California to trade for mules for export to the Boer War—a venture that nets him a seventy-five-thousand-dollar return on a seventeen-hundred-dollar investment—Zack falls in love with Inez, the "laughing-eyed" daughter of a Spanish grandee whose ranch was headquartered in San Juan Capistrano. Gipson describes her as "a live, proud thing, all fire and laughter and beauty" (pp. 174, 175). After a duenna fails to keep Zack and Inez apart, the grandee sends his daughter to Spain, obliterating all traces of her that Zack could follow.

> Inez was gone. And a part of Zack gone with her.
>
> Zack told himself he'd find her yet someday, but he never did.
>
> In 1904, Zack married a girl named Mabel Pettijohn. . . . They lived together six years and had one daughter . . . before the marriage went on the rocks. In 1919, Zack married again. . . . But that marriage didn't take either.
>
> Here and there Zack tried another woman or two. It never worked; always, there was something missing. (Pp. 179–80)

By 1905, the 101 Ranch Wild West Show started to bolster the sagging resources of the cattle operation. Selling day-to-day skills that the ranch hands practiced to run the 101 culminates a tendency that Zack Miller, now styled Colonel, had manifested since childhood when he negotiated with a medicine man to sell soft drinks to young braves undergoing painful initiations into manhood. The show toured all the major North American urban centers, steamed to Europe, and required enough logistical support to move a battalion of cavalry.

But despite oil discoveries on the 101 Ranch, the outfit was running out of resources. A flood of the Arkansas and Salt Fork in 1922 nearly wiped out the ranch headquarters, which by this time included a family residence called the White House that sheltered two hundred people during the flood. "The flood kept rising," Gipson wrote, "picking up horses, cows, buffaloes, chickens" (p. 358). Caught between the miles of flooding waters, the Miller brothers emptied the ranch's commissary to feed ranch workers, neighboring farmers, and stranded travelers. "'By God, old Noah didn't have much on us,'" Zack's brother, Col. Joe Miller exclaimed. At the height of the flood, the ranch put a ferry into operation, and ran it for the next eighteen months, replacing a lost bridge. Zack Miller told Gipson the ferry cleared twenty-five thousand dollars–"about what the 101 had lost to the flood in the first place" (p. 362). After the flood, the ranch limped along, no longer able to remain solvent through profits from diversified interests. Tastes shifted and crowds no longer filled coliseums to watch the Wild West Show. On the edge of bankruptcy, the whole family operation crumbled after the stock market crash in 1929. All the brothers except Zack died, and his thoughts inclined toward the "last frontier" of Africa if he could wrap his own affairs up with enough for passage for himself and one of the loyal ranch hands. Another of the 101 cowboys had gone to Africa years before: "the bronc-fanning, banjo-picking Ida Red–quitting one step ahead of John Laws, and riding out of their lives forever" (p. 379). Zack wrote to Ida Red to prepare for the arrival of the tag-ends of the 101.

> Zack folded and sealed the letter, a deep nostalgia making an ache come to his throat. Back in the days when Ida Red had been

> with the 101, a man's enemies had been flesh-and-blood creatures, something you could fight with fists and guns. Now that was all changed. Today, those enemies were signatures on a bank note, parties of the first and second parts in a contract, vague pen-and-ink names on legal documents that a gun or fist couldn't dent. (P. 379)

What he had despised to master as a boy—"booklearning" and "authority" (p. 59)—would bring him down in the end. For such foes his father, the Ponca chief, and the Irish crew boss had not prepared him.

Ida Red wrote back from British East Africa. "'She's the kind of country for grass and water that the Cherokee Strip was in the days your daddy tied into it. . . . The antelope are just as thick, and the lions thicker than the coyotes ever was in Oklahoma. But a man can raise cattle here—lions or no lions'" (p. 383). Red had a "fresh-water lake that never went dry," and he promised a good future for his old boss (pp. 383–84). "That letter . . . warmed Zack's heart, put new life and hope into his sick body. . . . It'd be like old times again. Zack wasn't old—only fifty-four. Given a little hope, and he'd soon be a damned sight younger" (p. 384). But Ida Red died. His wife wrote back to Zack to tell him of Ida Red's death.

> The last escape route for Zack Miller was gone now. There'd be no new frontiers for him; there was nobody to help him get a start in a new country. It was back off and start over, with nothing but his two bare hands, or tuck his tail and admit that he was done for good. . . . When a man's outlived his time, Zack would tell himself, all doors are closed to him. And a trainload of money wouldn't buy back the 101 and make it what it once was. The type of men who'd built it were gone, the horses, the longhorn cattle, the open range. That way of life was gone. (Pp. 409–10)

The book concludes with a symbolic device that may have had some currency for Gipson as well as for Col. Zack Miller. In a museum in the state capital hangs a buffalo hide with the names of the original four hundred members of the Cherokee Strip Cowpunchers' Association. Whenever a member died, a star was branded by his name. "Any time now, Zack would tell himself, they'd be burning a star beside his name—and he was ready" (p. 410).

The themes recurring from the Recollection Creek stories to *Fabulous Empire* are interwoven in all Gipson's writings. The first of these is the land, the setting, and invariably its state of decline. Gipson believed that the beauty of the land was once visible, but in the present (whenever that present is) it exists in the mind of the beholder, especially if the beholder can remember.[10] The second is good luck, closely associated with time; such luck can be depended upon only to go away. Individuals, realizing that sooner or later the "game will be up" and they will have to "go for broke," must "gather while they may." Third, women are like good luck, and a man must seize love when he can. Even if a man successfully hunts and captures the one true love, time may take love from him. Fourth, in order to win one last time against time, a man will need to sell his past or himself. He may turn his cowhands into a rodeo show, himself into a shibboleth of the past; but he will have to sell what he is trying to save. Fifth, he will comfort himself with the dream of a new frontier, but his problem will be getting there. If only he had anything left in reserve, he might even then have won.

Writing *Fabulous Empire* permitted Gipson to live Zack Miller's life vicariously and to see his own aspirations outlined against the backdrop of an outside world that reaffirmed, even intensified, his feelings of closure and entrapment.

The more constricted Gipson felt, viewing himself moving forward, the more he must have turned to two related but not entirely congruous solutions. One was a simple desire to flee into the Texas past, to a time even earlier than his birth—if possible, as far back as when the forerunners of civilization first looked up the valleys of the Llano and James rivers and Comanche Creek: when the fall from greatness began.

His other solution, the one to which he tried to hold himself after his final move back to Mason County—with wife and two sons now—was to migrate toward his own kind of future, a longstanding characteristic of the Hill Country Germans in the nineteenth century as well as of the "backward progress" in John Graves's *Hard Scrabble* more than a hundred years later.

This picture of time seems, for Gipson, to signal a new purpose, or ethic, of himself as a writer. Gipson's subsequent writings—from *Hound-Dog Man* to *Old Yeller*—remain consistent with that ethic. Like Miller, Gipson tried to help the land recover from spoliation. Like Miller, too, Gipson must have realized, *if* his thoughts were consistent with his writing, that he preferred retreat over marshaling the land's resources to meet future needs. He wanted the land as it had once been—restored to grassland, as he started several years later to do with his own land. The older he became, the more he pursued this vision with fervor, battling neighbors and fighting the drought of the 1950s that threatened to spoil his work.[11] But that is a preview, and in 1946 Gipson had not yet come to the awareness that angling into the future on his own terms was not a permanent way to make a deal with time.

Hound-Dog Man (1947) confirms and amplifies Gipson's "deal." The third work of Gipson's richly creative period in the 1940s, *Hound-Dog Man* became a movie in 1958—Gipson's third.[12] *Hound-Dog Man* was Gipson's favorite, as well as his most joyous and peaceful book. As a novel, it was far more unified and less didactic than the stories of Recollection Creek, finally published as a novel in 1955. Blackie Scantling, played in the movie by the singer Fabian when first-choice Elvis Presley was drafted into the U.S. Army, is a memorable Gipson characterization—

an outdoorsman firmly rooted in the landscape, a dark-haired beauty who, like Inez in *Fabulous Empire,* colors the world around him. One of the mothers of the community admits that Blackie is "cute as a bug" but warns her daughter, "'No woman can hold him. He's a prowler!'"[13] Comfortable outdoors, he has "'got plumb out of the habit of setting on a chair since Ma died'" (p. 13). When he spends the night at a married friend's home, he sleeps on the floor in front of the fireplace. "He said he'd got out of the habit of sleeping on a soft bed, anyhow; he'd laid out in the woods too many nights. He said he'd had an old bedstead his Ma had left him when she died, but he'd finally broke it up and burned it for firewood, just to keep it out from underfoot" (p. 21).

Although the story focuses on a hunt when Blackie initiates the son of his friend to the woods—"'You think a baby coon can set in his den and learn to catch a frog?'" (p. 18)—the moral of this idyll is that to win the love he decides he must have, Blackie will have to marry and sleep in a real bed again. As Fiddling Tom, the father of the girl, recollects with nostalgia, "'There's a time when a boy can lay his belly on the ground and feel the heartbeats of the earth coming up to him through the grassroots. That's his time to prowl . . . to hear the wind singing what's on the yonder side of the next ridge'" (p. 141). Such men, Fiddling Tom's wife and daughter know, make the finest husbands. But when that time has passed, it takes special women to bring them back and keep them in the folds of community. Young Cotton Kinney returns from the woods initiated, but he loses Blackie. He will someday come to know this time again. *Hound-Dog Man* is Gipson's most bittersweet tale, Blackie's compromise the closest thing Gipson wrote to a truly happy ending.[14]

CHAPTER FOUR

"A Good Dream" 1950–1953

In the bright winter sunlight, the hills appeared drab and lifeless. But to Sam Crockett, driving a jeep with its overloaded trailer along the twisting country lane, they were full of beauty and stirring with life.

THE HOME PLACE

With the Recollection Creek period of the late 1940s settling, Fred Gipson's writing seemed to become more "full of beauty and stirring with life."[1] A severe drought was starting in the 1950s in the Hill Country, but Gipson fought back by envisioning "a good dream." He argued with pictures and moods to demonstrate ideas. More and more, memory improved on experience during the scorching, dry years when Gipson's conservation efforts came to nothing and ranchers were grateful for the prickly-pear cactus so they could burn off the thorns and feed the nutritious, succulent plants to livestock. As he set out against increasing odds to reconstruct the "natural state" of the land, so too he tried to protect what he conceived as the ideal or utopian state of existence, however "drab and lifeless" it might have seemed to others.

He raised walls around the mythical community of Recollection Creek with three books told from an adult's view. *The Home Place* (1950) opens onto a drying landscape. With different characters and set some twenty-five years after *Hound-Dog Man,* the narrative brings a man like Gipson—or like a grown-up Hopper Creech or Cotton Kinney—back from the city to his native world. *Big Bend: A Homesteader's Story* (1952) records a family's pilgrimage from a world where the father is not well to one where father and family become healthier and happier. *Cowhand: The Story of a Working Cowboy* (1953), the biography of Fat Alford, presents ranch life in realistic detail but is still somewhat romanticized as a homily of homeliness. *Big Bend* and *Cowhand* are based on life stories, but the distinction between history and fiction being faint, it is not surprising to find these books only slightly less fictional than the novel, *The Home Place,* which may be read as another part of the Fred Gipson autobiography.[2] The theme of "going home," literally or figuratively, unites the novel and two biographies.

The Home Place, filmed as *The Return of the Texan* (1952), is Gipson's preeminent "place book," to use John Graves's description of *Hard Scrabble,* and in many ways *The Home Place* is like *Hard Scrabble.*[3] Gipson's novel is set in the late 1940s in a part of the Texas Hill Country that a later writer from Mason County said "does not yield wealth easily."[4] The story of a Texan named Sam Crockett, whose wife has recently died and who has returned with his three sons and his Grandpa Firth to the abandoned farmhouse where he grew up, *The Home Place* traces the precarious struggle of this family to survive on the eroded dry-land farm until the father marries Ann Marshall, a woman who can ride and fence and hunt. From a distance, and in retrospect, the story of the Crocketts is romantic, though abounding in realistic details, much in the way that the novel explores the ramifications of loving ideas and generalizations of things which, when one has them, become tiring and tiresome. As in many country and western tales, pathos dominates memorable passages: from a fateful day when pigs discover a way into a field of watermelons already optioned for money that would cover that year's mortgage to the day the youngest son attacks a rattlesnake and is bitten. Narration alternates with description, the landscape at times becoming animated, benign but hardly benevolent. Gipson's romantic realism, so overwhelming in this novel, is consistent with the Crockett family's search for a wilderness to inhabit: they recognize a contradiction between their goal and their ideal of the land restored to virginity. Characteristic of most of Gipson's works, this dual vision extends beyond the novel into the writer's life and foreshadows his future on such subjects as jobs, women, neighbors.[5]

The Home Place opens as the family winds into the setting along dry dusty roads, where dust lingers on fence posts, trees, and browning autumn pastures.

> Here were the hills, high-pitched against the sky, with rims sharp-edged and broken. Here were the short draws, the deep, narrow canyons, the tight little valleys. Scrub cedar combed the ridge tops. A ragged covering of prickly pear, agarita, catclaw, black persimmon and scrub mesquite lay over the rumpled slopes, and through the tattered holes in the brush, the bare rock ledges stood out like the weathered ribs of some prehistoric monster. Live oaks, huge of trunk and with gnarled branches infinitely graceful, stood in the valleys. Willows and cottonwoods leaned over plunging streams and clear pools of water. (P. 1)

The father, Sam, is "excited about coming back to the hills," but he is "no wide-eyed tenderfoot." In his late thirties, he realizes "that the Big Adventure no longer lies ahead" (p. 2).

"Yet the mood was on him, and the deeper he drove into the hills, the keener grew his anticipation" (p. 2). His spirit infects all the little family, even though their "old brownstone house . . .

constructed at a time when houses were built to last for generations" is, when they arrive, occupied by an indolent cow and a newborn calf, the front-yard gate is "wrecked" (p. 4), and the grass roots have been grazed "right out of the ground" (p. 5). Sam tells himself that he "had to be right" and he is "depressed by the realization that he might be wrong" (p. 6), but the family's gravest concerns leave them after Sam builds their first fire.

> Kneeling on the hearth before the fireplace, he took his time and did a careful job of splitting the board with his axe. He cut shavings from the smaller pieces with his pocket knife. . . .
>
> To Sam, who had often performed the age-old ritual of building a fire, there was something sobering and almost sacred in the act. (Pp. 11–12)

He later takes his sons to the county seat, Loma, "a Texas hill-country town . . . the usual aggregation of grocery stores, garages, filling stations, clothing stores, lumber yards, and 'greasy spoons,' some of which also served as juke-box honky-tonks for midnight prowlers" (p. 20). The people "speculate on the weather, which had a tendency toward extremes." They were "typical hill-country people"—"heroically patriotic" during times of war and "loudly contemptuous" during times of peace—but what made all the difference in the world for Sam, and eventually for his sons, was that Loma was home: "an embodiment of memories. . . . You . . . hardly see it in reality; you see it in relation to . . ." time. "On the surface, your home town may look like any other town anywhere. But beneath that surface lies an altogether different world—a world of memories from your youth" (pp. 21, 22). With all the pleasant and bittersweet recollections come also memories that arouse old antagonisms. Rod Murray, a rancher married into the old, five-thousand-acre Marshall spread and living in one of the massive multistory stone houses which abound in the real Mason County and which would have made any Scottish border laird proud, reminds Sam Crockett of how Sam's day-laborer father, Solomon Crockett, "used to brag on his work." Sam admits he does not know why hearing that story told should "irritate" him. "He knew his father for what he'd been, a dirt-poor 'peckerwood,' a little ridiculous in his stubborn, stiff-necked pride, yet a kind, honest man . . ." (pp. 33–34).

Sam Crockett's heightened sensitivity extends to the setting as well. He "got a heart-wrenching pleasure out of seeing his quarry escape" when he hunted (p. 34). He thinks "'most people who have grown up on the land never get away from it'" (p. 62). Being in the country frees his mind to "take note" of life, to attune his body and mind to his surroundings.

> When you're working outdoors and you have done your work till it has become a performance of rhythmic movements, then you can detach your mind from it and enjoy nature, plan your plans and dream your dreams—and still know when quitting time comes and your shadow lies long on the grass, that the job has been done as it should have been done; yet you can't for the life of you recollect just when or how you did any part of it. (P. 67)

These words describe the experience of person and style and vision and purpose fusing into one motion. Sam Crockett, who has learned, he thinks, to condition and to protect himself, worries about his older son Steve, blond and gray-eyed, solemn as Sam once was, "too shy, too sensitive, too easily hurt" (p. 66). His middle son, Chuck, apparently taking after the deceased mother, is "round-faced, brown-eyed, intent" (p. 4). The youngest son, Yo-Yo, is a would-be feral child who even at three years is pretty much in charge of himself. When Yo-Yo, bitten by a rattlesnake, drops into a coma from which he barely recovers near the end of the novel and Sam's old Grandpa Firth dies returning empty-handed from a hunt, the family regains a new wife and mother—the sensitive but tough and wealthy Ann Marshall from the neighboring ranch.

The family structure in the Crockett home interestingly—and, in retrospect, troublingly—parallels Gipson's own domestic life in 1950. His older son, Phillip Michael, then ten years old, was a sensitive boy who would become a campus activist at the University of Texas in the early 1960s. An aspiring writer, he ended his life in 1962 on his younger brother's birthday, which coincided that year with Father's Day. Fred Gipson's younger son, Thomas Beckton, was five in 1950. A child had been lost in 1946, and another would be lost in 1953. Gipson's wife Tommie was alive, however, as was Gipson's widowed mother Emma, who may stand as the real-life counterpart of Sam Crockett's Grandpa Firth. The Gipsons had just moved back to Mason County again in 1948 for the third time since their marriage in 1940, returning this time from Colorado where Gipson had taken a promising position that he soon came to dislike. Tommie Gipson's poor health after her marriage to Fred Gipson contrasts, however, with Ann Marshall's strength and confidence. But the drought and the landscape and the town of Loma are closely based on the Hill Country and Mason, and Rod Murray, husband of the older Marshall sister, could be based on any number of local ranchers—as the Marshall family may derive from such Hill Country German dynasties as von Marschall zu Bieberstein, von Meusebach, von Donop, Geisweidt, or Kothmann.

Critics, literary agent, and publisher were correct in seeing *The Home Place* as a departure from Gipson's earlier trilogy, but the book is consistent with the conclusion of *Hound-Dog Man* that women knit the fabric of community, and it is consistent in imagery, characterization, and theme with the corpus of Gipson's work. The books of this period in Gipson's writing depart from his earlier and later works mainly in that they are told from adult points of view and show Gipson's struggle to "grow up" as a writer and thinker and to find his way between the world of adults and of youth.

While in some ways *The Home Place* affirmed—or seemed in 1950 to affirm—the promise of the rural community and traditional folk values, Gipson's imagery for Sam Crockett's return from Kansas City seems as troubled by night as it seems reassuring by day.

> When night came at home in Kansas City, you were aware of the darkness, of course. It lay all about you, yet never quite touched you; always, there were lighted windows, street lamps, neon signs and the headlights of passing cars to keep it shoved back. There at night, you lived within the light and looked out into the darkness. But here in the woods, night came up to envelope you like a blanket, so that you lived in it and looked out at night. And the only light came from the high-hung stars. (P. 96)

While one cannot dispel a sense of nighttime closure and diminution, Gipson insists that during the day the hills "sing" (p. 189) and that *The Home Place* could have been "a good dream."

> You get yourself a dream. It is a good dream. It may lack the grace and beauty of the more fanciful dreams you had in your younger days, but it has one thing the others seldom had—a chance to stand. Rest this dream on the solid foundation of experience and reason which you now have, limit its scope to the realm of your abilities, and it could become a reality.
>
> So you set about making it so. . . . You choose only that material which is without flaw. . . .
>
> Any dream built in such a manner has to stand. Yet, long before the structure is complete, this one has buckled and collapsed. Because, from the very beginning, you ignored one thing—the human element.
>
> So there your dream lies, a heap of shattered rubble, just like the other heaps marking the sites of so many other dreams. Only,

> somehow, you can't just turn your back and walk away from this one as you did the others. Because you know, too, that this dream is your last one. (P. 222)

A note of eternal sadness pervades this novel, which begins with retreat and ends with the family barely surviving, and which identifies Gipson personally not with what remains but instead with what is lost.[6] Gipson's conclusion that "the only thing you're ever sure of is the fact that life is precious and hadn't ought to be wasted" (p. 243) allays but does not stay the tide of despair which on some readings overwhelms the novel, thought it may obliquely say something about Gipson's tensions and deeper feelings.

Gipson worried about what should follow the considerable popularity of *Hound-Dog Man* and *The Home Place,* which also became a bestseller and a book club selection and then almost immediately went into production as a movie. He tried to write a sequel to *Hound-Dog Man,* but supporters found the work lacking, probably because it is impossible to write a sequel to an *ending,* however much it masquerades as a new beginning. By this time suffering from recurring depression, Gipson accepted an offer to rewrite the autobiography of J. O. Langford, who had homesteaded in the Big Bend country in 1909.[7] Under the sponsorship of Henry B. Du Pont and the University of Texas Press, Gipson worked with Langford to bring the old homesteader's story to life. Gipson's selection for the job was almost coincidental, except that Frank Wardlaw of the University of Texas Press no doubt typecast Gipson as the personality who could refine the Langford story. *Big Bend* turned into another loosely autobiographical biography, as had occurred with *Fabulous Empire.* In the process of selecting material to heighten the story, Gipson made explicit passages that had been implicit in Langford's draft.[8]

Not quite the self-fulfilling prophecy of *Fabulous Empire*, and not well written, *Big Bend* nonetheless catalogs themes and conventions that repeat themselves from one Gipson work to another. The plot is Gipson's familiar one of the individual against time. A family sets out on a quest for a "fantastic country" that will cure the ills of the father.[9] Their gamble leaves nothing in reserve: "One serious accident, and we'd go under" (p. 5).

Far more barren than Mason County, the Big Bend seemed a "damned country that promises more and gives less than any place" Langford had seen (p. 7). An old German had tried to homestead it and finally gave up: "'He couldn't stand it. No man in his right mind would try homesteading down there, anyway. Too lonesome!'" (p. 8). Still the family pushed on, despite the warning at each outpost, always smaller than the last, of how desolate and forsaken their destination was. Moving through a landscape of incredible scale and pellucid air, Langford remembers that they found in the land "something compelling and mysterious that grips you the first time you see it and never afterward leaves you" (p. 28). They learned to live with the vicissitudes of fate and to imitate the calm trust (making "much of life and little of death" [p. 55]) of the sparse local population whose ancestry extended back through the thousands of years that people had clung tenuously but tenaciously to the sides of these valleys. The Langfords' "fervent" quest was rewarded ultimately when the father recovered his health. Together, Anglo Americans and Mexicans transformed their valley into a garden of health. A hot mineral spring healed them and attracted others who sought cures there, evoking not only the myth of the fountain of youth but also the myth that every land would produce cures for its own particular illnesses.[10] But whereas the Mexicans were satisfied to keep to themselves or to give to the needy what they had chanced upon, Langford knew "there should be some way that a man of ingenuity could cash in on it" (p. 46).

Over the long run, however, time and bad luck blighted his prospects.

Political unrest and revolution on the Mexican side of the river spread lawlessness into the little valley where the Langfords lived. Pancho Villa raids forced them to move to El Paso "until the trouble on the Rio Grande was over" (p. 152). When they returned after the war, they found abandoned dwellings, their "roofs fallen in," where once had lived "a happy and prosperous family"—the people "starved out by the blind greed and ignorance of men who had changed their paradise into a desert wasteland." The Langfords left again and returned next in 1927, and they tried from then until 1942 to remake what had been lost, selling their precious mineral waters in order to restore paradise. Langford admits they prospered. "Yet, never again did we have that which we'd had in the beginning. Somehow, the brightness seemed gone from the land" (p. 154).

Before Gipson finished, *Big Bend* had become tedious, and the last chapters are relatively threadbare, Gipson having tired of the project with Langford.[11] The book presents an alter ego, though, to a persistent myth in American history. In 1893 Frederick Jackson Turner had announced his famous frontier thesis that rugged individualism had been the way of American life. *Big Bend* counters that view in much the way that Gipson's acquaintance, folklorist Mody Boatright, argued in an essay entitled "The Myth of Frontier Individualism" (1941).[12] Boatright contended that a significant portion of the frontier experience was predicated upon cooperative collectivism. Boatright and Gipson insist on setting a record straight—on putting the individual back into the group. While Gipson's characters often look like "rugged individualists," their success occurs within or as they move into community—in this case a binational, bicultural community. That theme was emergent in Gipson's writings at this time and toward the end of his life became more pronounced.

So too Gipson's picture of the real western cowboy combines rugged individualism with cooperative collectivism. Like Boatright, who wrote an essay entitled "The American Myth Rides the Range" (1951), Gipson was fascinated with the cowboy and wanted to paint him in the true colors of Russell instead of those of Remington.[13] In undoing the Hollywood travesty of America's only truly indigenous hero, the biography of Fat Alford recorded in Gipson's *Cowhand* is nonetheless a galloping picaresque tale. "The truth can be as romantic as the most imaginative myth," Gipson's young East Coast editor at Harper's explained in the foreword.[14]

Cowhand is stock Gipson—the third work in the triad to which it belongs—filled with familiar conventions and written to make money from familiar materials. Focusing on what C. L. Sonnichsen describes as the unheroic cowboy in western fiction, *Cowhand* has been variously faulted for supposed inaccuracies or praised, in the case of Tom Lea, as "excellent" in its portrayal of the true cowboy.[15] That has been the height of the criticism. The action is set in "a man-size country" (p. 8). The landscape (we already know) is "a fantastic country. High, bald ridges. . . . Crawling desert sands. Gushing springs, some hot, some cold. Salt lakes. . . . Flat-topped mesas. Deep tortuous canyons. Great desert plains sweeping up to pine-studded mountains, and the mountains standing blue in the distance" (p. 9). As is clear from this landscape description, Gipson has written this material before. The themes here confirm his earlier writings. He is troubled by no new questions, and the style is smooth. As *Hound-Dog Man* shows a kind of conclusion to Gipson's Recollection Creek period, so *Cowhand* suggests an end to this part of Gipson's career in the early 1950s.

In *The Home Place, Big Bend,* and *Cowhand,* Gipson postulated a time from about 1901 until the late 1940s when problems were surmountable, even if only through retreat and consolidation of resources. Two or three generations later than the times commonly associated with America's pioneering history, Gipson's characters are pioneers of another sort who seek out frontiers bypassed during the westward movement. In their sequestered valleys, folk virtues assure survival, if not rain. The main characters—Sam Crockett and sons, the Langford family, and Fat Alford—represent some of the major archetypes of American pioneer fiction, but they are archetypes reduced to a diminished present. Heroic in their own ways as overland explorers, cowboys, and prairie farmers, Gipson's heroes are silent men tamed by the realization that whatever gold is in their hills will sustain them and theirs only if marshaled with caution.[16] These people do not tower over their surroundings, though their surroundings are dwarfed and appear grand only to the remembering eye. Their stories are elegies of loss—typical pioneer tales of men and nature, conflict and luck—but their purpose is to modernize scattered elements of myth into archetypes once coherent but, in the 1950s, threatened.[17] Working in his own way within what Claude Lévi-Strauss has called "a verbal tradition, which is claimed to be history," Gipson salvaged what he thought was the true story of his time. Nowhere is this imperative more obvious than in *Cowhand,* with its collection of episodes from a working cowboy's long (and tedious) life into a kind of testament. Lévi-Strauss cites such collections as attempts to gather the virtues of the past, in the same way that the genealogies of dynastic heirs attempt to collect inheritance: "as if a diachronic succession of events was simultaneously projected on the screen of the present in order to reconstitute piece by piece a synchronic order which exists and is illustrated by the roster of names and privileges of a given individual."[18]

Cowhand is another of Gipson's attempts to reconstitute order. Truth, Gipson writes in his introduction to *Cowhand,* is "a far cry" from "Hollywood standards" (p. xi), but his cowboys have "a way of meeting life head on, with a recklessness and a wildness of spirit and a real relish for conquering it. They go after life "as if it were something that had to be roped in a hurry before it got away" (p. xii). The imagery is consistent with Gipson's earlier writings, if not with his life. What Gipson does share with his characters is an attitude toward time as the sure medium of decline and destruction rather than as the dimension or, more romantically, the frontier of opportunity, as in the American myth. Willing to capture the perfect moment with violence, Gipson tries to "bulldog" history and tie it into what he wants, actively engaging the rituals of social reality through a medium as homely as, say, a patchwork quilt. His disclaimer in *Cowhand* that "a good tale . . . doesn't need to prove or signify anything" is a formulaic part of the convention, or a way of dealing with critics, perhaps not to be believed any more seriously than the claims of a hunter regarding the prowess of a dog he is trying to sell.[19] Gipson wanted a future that would remain faithful to what he liked from the past, which was also what he wanted out of the land.[20]

As a raconteur or storyteller, Gipson shoulders the burden of preserving, transmitting, and administering tradition. This tradition has a precarious coherence, subject to loss through drought, erosion, aging, and death. Only as its objects themselves endure, as artifacts and memories, do the traditions that attach to them last.[21] Since these symbols always come in sets, whole and extensive bodies of meaning are transported in mindscapes that emerge functionally and structurally in these three works.

Fred Gipson is not a simple storyteller as much as he is a simplifying one—with a strong accent on the sense of process in that word. The germ of his writing is the world remembered, little kernels he combined and rearranged and reused with some variety but always with an attempt, it seems, to speak "through things and through the medium of things," as Lévi-Strauss describes the behavior of the bricoleur.[22] This crafting of meaning—simultaneously engendering and being engendered, at once inside and outside—marks Gipson as a true bricoleur: a maker of meanings from second-hand tales, finding new futures for old things, shuffling names, and attributing new natures and new groupings in a kind of ongoing improvisation. Akin to revisionist and relativist history, or to neighborhood gossips setting the record straight as to what really should have happened, bricolage is a poetic, folk-forming, fiction-forming activity in the tradition of the courtly bard but not at all unlike most writing of literature and probably much of history as well.

Operating out of a strong imperative to point and motivate, Gipson was not blind to the potential of tales like *The Home Place, Big Bend,* and *Cowhand* to speak to, or simplify, or interpret values. Yet because of its simplicity, his writing has been misunderstood and underestimated.[23] But a country and western tale, like a modern "primitive" painting, can criticize through its very simplicity. Such criticism is heightened when the works are placed within their often regional contexts, and when those contexts in turn are seen within the national context. The socioeconomic and political milieu that produced the flat illustrational realism of American Scene artists also produced Gipson, and it is hardly surprising that such painters and Gipson speak about the same nation, albeit from different regions. In *The Home Place, Big Bend,* and *Cowhand,* as well as in his later works, Gipson interprets behavior, society, history, and values—the consistent subjects of American farm novels in the twentieth century.[24] He reflects on, and sometimes sentimentalizes, the social construction of reality, not only of a world as it was, but also of a world as it perhaps ought to become. He judges the collective whole, the body politic, using the past in much the way that a cartoonist may use the present moment. Critics do not miss the often overt statement of cartoons, nor do they deny ballads a power to lament and complain – and criticize – even though the balladeer sings through a mask. Like the country and western songs of Gipson's Texas, the stories of Fred Gipson are rooted in an implicitly critical tradition that speaks obliquely through style and content, "through things and through the medium of things."

CHAPTER FIVE

"Memories Are Long" *1956*

"What if our animals do have the sickness?" The People charged. "Does an infirmity justify murder?"

So the people resisted; and they were a people with a long experience in resisting.

They applied a term of sly derision to members of La Comisión, *calling them* los matavacas *("the cow killers"), the implication being that they gloried in killing female cattle for lack of courage to face a bull in the ring.*

"THE COW KILLERS"

To readers familiar only with Fred Gipson's juveniles, or with such gentle tales as the Recollection Creek stories, "*The Cow Killers*" (1956) comes as an abrupt surprise, differing from Gipson's other writings as much as a Thomas Hart Benton painting differs from one by Grant Wood, for example. The writing is terse, epigrammatic. The tone is reserved, but the reticence speaks eloquently of sympathy and wisdom in the face of conflict, of individualism and collectivism conjoined in a particularly vernacular setting.

Written in collaboration with artist Bill Leftwich, "*The Cow*

Killers" shows one of the directions in which Gipson's writing inclined and in which it might have continued. Composed in short sketches and vignettes, these little studies suggest enough setting and action that the plots and themes are completed in the reader's mind, resonating in experience, with the language coming alive and a rich choreography of gesture enacting the ethos of what Gipson and Leftwich call "The People."

The crafting of the pieces is what one would expect from no other Texas writer except Katherine Anne Porter, for here Gipson and the Porter of the Mexico years are alone among major Texas writers.[1] It seems therefore unfortunate that "*The Cow Killers*" was a kind of last flowering of Gipson's talent. When it was written, his two best juveniles, *The Trail-Driving Rooster* (1955) and *Old Yeller* (1956), were already completed. He wrote one more significant novel, *Savage Sam* (1962)—the third of the juvenile triad and derivative of the first two, as was customary with Gipson—and left two short pieces, *Little Arliss* (1978) and *Curly and the Wild Boar* (1979), both published posthumously.

Occasioned by the sketches of Bill Leftwich, "*The Cow Killers*" is a fortunate accident of Texas literature. Bill Leftwich, a native of West Texas and a resident of Fort Davis, served in World War II, then attended Texas A&M, and in 1949, accompanied by his wife and child, went to Mexico to fight hoof-and-mouth disease as a livestock inspector for the Aftosa Commission. After work, he would record his vivid impressions in line and wash, creating a cartoonlike record of confrontations between the commission and the soldiers protecting it ("arrogant Mexican officials of the ruling *gente decent* class, equally arrogant Texans, New Mexicans, and Arizonans") and The People (indigenous Yaquis who hated the *conquistadores* who for nearly four centuries had "robbed the native, beaten him, starved him, and held him in contempt").[2]

In addition to creating these drawings, done in a spare style reminiscent of Benton's, Leftwich wrote accompanying notes that he later shared with Gipson. These notes evoked a strong response in Gipson, who already believed that oppression is wrong, that the uprising of the oppressed leads to a new oppression, that only through synthesis will a lasting good come into being. The two men enjoyed working together and shared their sympathies for the ultimate victims of the epidemic: the peasants. In the evenings Gipson learned all he could from Leftwich about parts of Mexico that Gipson did not know from his own visits to that country. He shared with Leftwich his dreams of living in Mexico and of writing the life of the simple peasant, close to the earth and with all parts of life balanced.

The Leftwich drawings focused much of what Gipson himself had seen and experienced into a powerful moral drive that expressed itself stylistically. Never having "learned the power of forgiveness," Gipson harbored his injuries—injuries sustained as a poor boy on a dry-land farm, growing up insecure and distrustful of women, as a farmhand who once struck a man so forcefully that he feared to have killed him, as a day-laborer on a road crew who raised a sledgehammer handle to the boss who had denied him his pay, as an awkward student, as a journalist who was refused a raise and then was fired because he would not write predictable feature stories, as an author driven to rage when he was told to delete the word *coon* from *Hound-Dog Man* because of its racial connotation, as a man who dreamed of restoring his homeplace but who saw it wasted, first by abuse, then by drought, and finally by neighbors whose pig farm's acrid odor sickened the family.[3] Always fighting for "place," figuratively or literally, he sustained an antagonism toward those who blocked him or denied him ingress. Two years earlier he had admitted in "The Road Leads West," the manuscript for a travel book rejected by Evan Thomas of Harper's as too bitter, that this "herd" was his enemy.

> Maybe I do have to fight it to exist, or rather fight against its fool laws that don't fit nature. The law says, "Be meek, be kind, be gentle," but when you try it, the whole herd steps in your face, hurrying past to pay tribute to the arrogant, the cruel and the selfish, because he's the boy who wins. He's got the money, the power, the rich estates, the fine whiskeys, the beautiful women. He's bound to be somebody.[4]

"*The Cow Killers*" provided a channel for release. Before five more years passed, however, Gipson's precarious world would collapse into assault and battery against the hog raisers, into alcoholism and shock treatments, and into the disintegration of his family. His health seriously deteriorated, his wife reporting that he sometimes writhed on the floor in agony. While writing in Hollywood he became incapacitated and his wife and Joe Small, his friend from Austin, were barely able to help him meet his contractual obligations. Besides worrying about movie scripts, Gipson was frustrated about conservation, at one point writing to President Johnson and blaming Washington for the problems he was having with his land program.[5]

In 1956, though, his world still held. For a writer, he knew it was an intensely creative period, and he used it to write both "*The Cow Killers*" and *Old Yeller,* which overshadowed "*The Cow Killers*". The two books complement each other and mirror their author's soul: alternately gentle and angry, always sensitive, always threatening to split apart. For the moment, the Leftwich drawings did for Gipson in "*The Cow Killers*" what the persona of childhood did for him in *Old Yeller:* they provided a way to focus on the perspective of the victims of time.

One of the technical feats of "*The Cow Killers*" is its point of view. Gipson uses three third-person limited voices: one for the agents of authority; a second, more frequent voice that represents The People; and a listener's point of view, which occasionally intrudes as an authorial voice, forms in the reader's thoughts.

Leftwich's drawings extend meaning, putting into images feelings about the masses that words alone cannot quicken. The interaction of these two media in "*The Cow Killers*" exerts a powerful effect on the audience.

Just as Leftwich's drawings mainly show The People, Gipson's narrative is told largely in the voice of The People. Their sentences are short. Their voice is flat, timeless, and haunting. They say only part of what they know. Their language is elastic, stretching to accommodate change through self-explaining compounds. The wording tends toward substantification and the sentences toward the passive and expletive, with prepositions used to build possessives that give the language a ponderous cadence.

The People are a collective, actively constituting themselves into a body, though always some members rise above others. These more prominent members of the collective are described in relation to the group as "The Old One," "The Lieutenant," "The Woman of Tzengio," and so on. Animals and authorities have names. But for a people "with long experience in resisting," names afforded no advantage: "The People neglected to corral their livestock for inspection. They hid them away in remote and secret canyons. They disclaimed ownership. They had no horses to hire out to members of *La Comisión*, no food to sell, no knowledge of the road leading to the house of a neighbor" (p. 6). From the moment of arrival in each peasant village, the commission would be met with resistance.

> *La Comisión* would . . . be directed to a house that was like all the other houses. . . .
>
> A gringo would knock at the door. The wife would come out, close the door behind her, and stand waiting, with prepared answers.
>
> "*Señora,* we seek the one in charge of order."
>
> "That is my husband, *señor;* but he is not present."
>
> "Where is he?"
>
> "He is gone."

"Where?"

"To the mountains, *señor,*" the wife would say, lifting a hand in a vague, directionless wave toward the range beyond.

"Is there a road into the mountains?"

"Yes. For the burros."

"When will your husband return?"

"Who knows?"

"Tonight?"

"It is possible. But it will be late. Of a certainty, it will be very late, should he return at all." (Pp. 7, 9)

Gipson writes that the commission then got directions to the house of the second in charge. That one could not read. "And how can a man be expected to follow orders when he cannot read the words?" (p. 9).

The Yaquis did not understand, and "often The People became confused" (p. 10). With their primitive ways, they exasperate members of the commission by mistaking coincidence and causation—or so the members of the commission think—by listening to rumor, and by clinging to superstition. Because of the virulent nature of hoof-and-mouth disease, the vaccinations of healthy cattle and shootings of already infected livestock proceed with dispatch. "So consuming was the desire of *los matavacas* to pick animals with their needles that they came even on fiesta days" was the word passed from village to village (p. 28).

"In Mexico there are too many fiesta days," the gringo complained.

"But *señor!*" the ranchero exclaimed, "that is impossible. On fiesta days, one may cease all labor. He may visit with his friends. He may drink. He may dine. He may dance. He may make love to the beautiful women. One does not work on fiesta days. How, then, can there be too many?" (P. 28)

Fighting ensued—"*when words fail, there is always the machete!*"—and the first pig to be vaccinated receives a cut meant for the gringo doctor. "As a result, the guests corralled the pigs, the host lay long unconscious, the slashed sow died, and the fiesta was completely spoiled" (p. 30). With such understatement, Gipson explains what Leftwich's sketches show: a world under attack by agents of forces The People cannot understand. Their old ways fail, and their holistic life crumbles. Happy before—the same people who make much of living but little of dying—they may never be happy again, though their herds will be healthy. They trade religion for security, and they are wise enough to know that in so doing, they lose.

Gipson writes with gallows humor. Paid for oxen that *La Comisión* exterminates, the farmers are forced to buy mules, because mules are immune to the disease that attacked cloven-hoofed animals.

> "But I know not the nature of a mule!"
>
> "You will learn."
>
> And The People did learn. They learned that the mule was an animal without patience. Beat him and curse him, and the beast fought back. He kicked and he bit. He took fright at all manner of foolish things and snorted and ran and tore down fences and wrecked harness and plows. And even when he was willing to follow the furrows, he walked too fast.
>
> . . . How one did long for the slow, patient gait of oxen—the pace of Mexico!
>
> Also there were times, after the oxen had been killed, when the mules were slow in arriving. Often, a fiesta day came first. . . .
>
> . . . Soon the mules are forgotten, the money is spent, and the one who once owned the finest yoke of oxen in Mexico sobers up in jail, with no oxen, no money, and no mules. (P. 33)

Gipson composes entire vignettes in dialogue on the feelings and character of The People. One story entitled "God's Own Little Pig" reveals profound pathos:

Near the village of Tiríndaro stood an ancient adobe-walled hut, roofed with short, overlapping sections of maguey blades. In the hut lived an Indian woman of so many years that The People called her "The Old One." With The Old One lived Chuchi, a spotted, long-snouted, diminutive pig.

The pig Chuchi filled that great place in the heart of The Old One left empty by the death of her man, by the loss of two sons to the army, and by the one daughter who worked in a *casa de putas* and seldom bothered to visit her mother.

Chuchi ate beans and tortillas with The Old One. At night he slept on the same floor mat, snuggling up against her withered breasts in a manner to remind her of that long-ago time when those breasts were full to bursting with milk for hungry babies. . . .

Chuchi was the one warm, living, breathing creature that stood between The Old One and the vast loneliness known to the old ones in every land.

Thus it was to be expected that when *La Comisión* came with its long and wicked needles The Old One rose up in defense of her beloved.

First she reasoned, then she pleaded, and finally, realizing the inevitable, she felt leap inside her a dark and terrible anger. Down from the low roof of the hut she snatched a scythe with a fresh-honed edge that glinted in the sunlight. Wheeling, she ran forward and placed herself between Chuchi and the soldiers. Standing there with the scythe raised threateningly, with her bare feet planted wide apart in the hot dust of Mexico's earth, she stared straight into the black bores of the rifles trained on her and cursed the soldiers and the gringos with a magnificent defiance.

"Dogs of dogs!" she charged them. "He-goats! Offspring of the Devil's whores! Would you murder God's own little pig?"

They would do even that!

While the soldiers, guns held ready, advanced upon her, a dog of a *matavacas* sneaked in from behind and snatched up the squealing Chuchi.

The Old One whirled with a scream of rage. The scythe flashed

"The Old One," by Bill Leftwich (courtesy Bill Leftwich)

a bright arc in the sunlight. But a hard-swung rifle barrel deflected the deadly blow and chopped The Old One down, felling her to the earth, where her screams all but drowned out the gasping squeals of the terrified Chuchi as the long needle drove under his skin.

When The Old One finally struggled to her feet, *los matavacas* were already departing. She ran after them a way, shouting curses

> and obscenities through the dust kicked up by the rubber-tired wheels. Then, weeping brokenly, she returned to gather the beloved Chuchi into her arms and await his death.
>
> By one of God's miracles, Chuchi lived, although for months afterward he wore a knot above one ear, a terrible knot, fully as large as one of The Old One's gnarled and broken-nailed thumbs. (Pp. 34, 36–37)

Leftwich's icon of The Old One, rock in one hand and sickle in the other, is as serious in intent as Gipson's portrait in words. Another vignette—accompanied by a Leftwich drawing of the same face of the folk, this time in profile—sounds the ethos of The People.

> "Our cattle shall not be murdered!" agreed The People of the village of Tzengio. They said to one another: "When *los matavacas* come, we will defend our livestock. We will gather in a great mob and fight with knives and pitchforks and scythes and stones. We will not permit *La Comisión* to slaughter our animals."
>
> The People were agreed and very determined.
>
> *La Comisión* came. The members arrived in an army power wagon. They were eight in number. There was a veterinarian, a captain of the army, a sergeant, a private first class, and four privates.
>
> When members of *La Comisión* encountered the sullen mob awaiting them in the town plaza, they stopped the truck. The captain got out. He lifted a hand in greeting and attempted to explain.
>
> "We have not come to kill your cattle," he assured The People. "We have not even brought our needles to pick them. We come only to inspect, to learn if your livestock has the sickness.
>
> The People were aroused with fear and hatred, but the words of the captain seemed fair. The men considered. Was the captain to be trusted?
>
> The old woman, Teodora Marta, saw their hesitancy and was ashamed. She cried out to the men in a taunting voice: "*Qué pasa, hombres?* Are you men—or he-goats?"

> Then she lunged forward and stabbed the captain in the chest with a huge knife.
>
> The first soldier was armed with an automatic rifle. He jammed a cartridge clip into the gun and brought it to his shoulder.
>
> But the mortally wounded captain cried out: "No! Do not shoot! Our orders are not to shoot!"
>
> The soldier hesitated. It was only for a moment, but after that it was too late.
>
> The men of the village were quick to act after the old woman had goaded them and opened the fight. They flung themselves upon the soldiers. They tore the guns from their hands. They stabbed them with knives. They dragged them to the ground and beat their heads with stones. They gouged the eyeballs from the sockets of the dead captain's head and mutilated the bodies of the others. . . .
>
> The People of Tzengio had agreed that their cattle should not be murdered. (Pp. 16, 18)

Arranged in a loose counterpoint, the sketches alternate in their message, the criticism heavily undercut by the stereotypical nonchalance of *mañana*-humor. Gradually the sharp edge of the titles grows dull—

> "Beware of the Needles!"
> "Of What Value Are Words?"
> "What Is the Remedy for Death?"
> "There Is Always Tomorrow"
> "Now They Are Shooting the People!"
> "The Man Who Smokes Like a Chimney"
> "A Fine Sense of Humor"

—or seems to dull. The titles of the last five sketches, however, shift almost imperceptibly in tone, but a reader grown sensitive to Gipson's symbology—his hierarchy of metaphors—senses the shift:

"Memories Are Long"
"A Matter of Politics"
"The Canyon of Death"
"A Reputable Assassin"
"Peace Is a Dream"

What has been implicit in Gipson's works in the twelve years between the Recollection Creek stories and the publication in 1956 of "*The Cow Killers*" and *Old Yeller* becomes overt here. Just as one is lulled into thinking the sweet dream that time will heal the psychic wounds of The People, Gipson introduces the theme of vengeance in a vignette entitled "Memories Are Long." One of The People owns a Cantina. He speaks English, and members of *La Comisión* like to frequent his establishment. He tells them he learned English in Chicago. Why was he there? He had killed a man and had gone away for a number of years to let passions cool. He has been back for a long time. Everyone has forgotten.

But one day, the dead man's kinsmen come, and they shoot the owner. No one escapes justice.

"Memories Are Long" is ominous, though the reader acknowledges that these are only poor people, barely human, eking out their existence from the shallow, dry soil. Then politics comes onto the stage—diminutively, but of the substance and of the nature of Politics—another name for what The People have endured for sixteen generations. The macabre "Canyon of Death" shows the assassination of a paid assassin, an Outsider who dies at the hands of one—of any—of The People. His death will remain unavenged. It is too expensive and too troublesome for the Government to pursue and prosecute. In the last sketch, "Peace Is a Dream," the mytho-logos of The People comes true as they witness what they intuited all along and expected to happen even before it happened.

Gipson is careful to undermine much of "*The Cow Killers*".

Written in a low style throughout, the collection of vignettes and sketches ends almost inaudibly. The subject at the end is smallpox. The final sketch, "Peace Is a Dream," includes two Leftwich drawings. The first seems overtly religious since it evokes the image of a priest's hands with chalice and broken wafer (bowl of *frijoles* and folded *tortilla*). Gipson's text concludes:

> "Do you prefer death from smallpox to the mere picking of a needle?" the officials demanded.
>
> The People did, and they said so, in no uncertain tones.
>
> But, of course, they were given no choice in the matter. In every town and village, at every crossroads and bus stop, The People were corralled by soldiers and inspected by women nurses. And unless they could display upon their arms the ugly scar that proved a previous vaccination, they were forced, under threat of armed soldiers, to submit to the needle.
>
> Apparently, for The People, the dream of peace is nothing more than a dream. (Pp. 128, 130)

Branded as chattel of the Government, The People are lucky they could be inoculated. They remember what happened to some of their cattle. The second Leftwich drawing closes the book with a view of a scrawny bull, tail thrown over its back, blood or saliva pouring from its mouth, standing silhouetted against the sky, no place to go.

Gipson is neither reductivist nor reactionary. The People are All People, and they are to be faulted for opposing something as good for them as smallpox vaccinations. The Government is benevolent in intention, if brusque in execution; the imperatives of progress and population permit no alternatives. Gipson addresses principles beyond those of The People versus Government, seeing irreparable losses for both and victory for neither. The virgin wilderness offered spiritual abundance, mystery, and action.[6] Things died and waste abounded, but continual regeneration transcended this violence of nature. Now The People will live longer, but they will lose religion, mystery, and happiness. Gipson laments the bifurcation of the self—into head versus heart, into modern versus traditional—and turned back history to write his juveniles.

"*The Cow Killers*" is not so much an exception in Gipson's career, as it is a significant text where structures which consistently guided his thoughts and values come to the surface. In "*The Cow Killers*" Gipson writes a kind of thesis literature. One might call it propagandistic, except that propaganda is seldom self-effacing and humorous.

CHAPTER SIX

"A Sort of Double Meaning" 1955–1965

We called him Old Yeller. The name had a sort of double meaning. One part meant that his short hair was a dingy yellow color, a color that we called "yeller" in those days. The other meant when he opened his head, the sound he let out came closer to being a yell than a bark.

OLD YELLER

Fred Gipson's sales record, especially with his juveniles, is one of the success stories of Texas literature. Of ten major works published during his lifetime, four became movies. Several of his books hit best-seller lists, and one—*Old Yeller* (1956)—sold more than three million copies in American and foreign editions before Gipson's death in 1973, securing Gipson's fame in the United States and abroad, so that today Gipson is remembered as a children's writer, as a man who could get inside a boy's head better than anyone else since Mark Twain.[1]

What he created most successfully during his short literary career of twenty years and what seem even today his most finished writings in terms of literary craftsmanship are his juveniles. A majority of his books—five of the ten major works published during his lifetime, or seven of the twelve longer works if the two posthumous novels are included—may be classified as children's literature and are widely cited as such. Two of these, *Recollection Creek* and *Hound-Dog Man,* are interesting and lively reading for young people but as the reminiscences of adults, are not juveniles in the strictest sense. Whether or not Gipson is rightly measured as mainly a writer of children's literature, he did select the juvenile as the vehicle for his final works, and having two popular Walt Disney movies to his credit, he has a secure place as a writer for young readers, the most popular such author Texas has produced.

Gipson's first true juvenile is *The Trail-Driving Rooster* (1955), dedicated to his sons, "Mike and Beck, that they may get one brief glimpse of their country as it once was."[2] Starting on the Nueces River in South Texas in 1881, this novella follows a cattle drive north to Dodge City, Kansas, during the boom years following the end of Reconstruction in the trans-Mississippi South and after the closing of the frontier, dated by the cessation of Indian raids and the advent of windmills. The second juvenile, *Old Yeller,* was made in 1957 into a Walt Disney movie that grossed eight million dollars in domestic box offices alone.[3] Set in the late 1860s, before windmills, and dedicated to Gipson's parents, *Old Yeller* is austere in style but rich in meanings. The novel traces the story of a boy's growth into manhood as a part of a larger story of a frontier family that survives only because every member works together. *Savage Sam* (1962), Gipson's third juvenile, was promoted as a sequel to *Old Yeller* both as a novel and as a Disney movie. Dedicated to all the dogs Gipson has known, *Savage Sam* includes recollections derived from his own childhood. The two other juveniles are the posthumously published *Little Arliss* (1978) and *Curly and the Wild Boar* (1979).[4]

In the three important children's novels—*The Trail-Driving Rooster, Old Yeller,* and *Savage Sam*—the familiar themes of time, conflict, initiation, strength, and ingenuity are portrayed without the filter of adult nostalgia.[5] As in "*The Cow Killers*", two kinds of violence are explored: first, a violence of wasteful, youthful, savage, tribal, and primitive nature, and second, a violence of scientific but dismembered history. Thus, a distinction becomes apparent between natural time and historical time. The juveniles have historical settings, but the main characters, the youngsters, are unaware of the earlier paradise from which the land has declined since the arrival of westering Americans and European colonists, whose coming marks the beginning of historical time.

Shifting from his earlier works which record a world continually dropping off from what might once have been, Gipson struggles in these later novels to engage his art in the crafting, not just of stories, but of narratives that catch the world while it is still growing up, that *convey* the essential self of a place and its people and *point* this symbolic self-portrait toward a more desirable future projected by the author.

The three major children's novels, like Gipson's other works, function both as social correctives and as personal messages. Returning in his older years to the scenes of childhood, Gipson here assumes the persona of a man leaving a testament. The message is significant but has been refined and simplified. The sequence of the dedications—to his children "that they might get one brief glimpse . . ." (1955), to his parents "whose memorable tales . . . of frontier dogs supplied . . . incident and background for this story" (1956), and to "some loyal and faithful companions . . . who helped make a Big Adventure . . ." (1962)—is important because in this trilogy Gipson charts the rhetorical thrust of his last writings. Both the past and the present suffer in the tension between nature and history. Gipson's oblique approach to the future accommodates some of the demands of history while retaining as much of nature as he can, a sometimes satisfactory balance in the juveniles. His audience shifts from adults remembering when they had been "more themselves than at any other time" to youth itself in *The Trail-Driving Rooster,* the legacy, more on the side of nature than of history, that he wanted his sons to inherit. Published in 1955, the year he published the stories of Recollection Creek as a novel, *The Trail-Driving Rooster* grows from the same nostalgia for a golden past that colors Gipson's nonjuvenile writings. This golden past—nature unspoiled by time, people uninhibited by history—flows from the Recollection Creek period starting in 1944 to *Fabulous Empire* in 1948 and "*The Cow Killers*" in 1956: a continuous, coherent emotion which Gipson personified most evocatively in the dog Old Yeller and in the unique and solitary character of Aaron Blood in Recollection Creek who no longer talks to adults but who hopes yet to guide the youth, not to spare them from but to help prepare them for the violence of nature and time.[6] Guided by Aaron Blood and attended by dogs, the young Creeches along Recollection Creek share much with the Coates family in *Old Yeller,* wherein Gipson preserves the "country as it once was," spoken into being through tales he knew from his parents.[7] In *Old Yeller,* the dog fuses the roles of guide and attendant, becoming a guardian. The dog's death at the end of the novel foreshadows loss of the symbolic utopia, whether the land of eternal youth or Ida Red's Africa. Given the metaphoric values of the dog and regardless of how necessary the dog's death becomes, the shooting remains an act of violence directed at the author's self.

Old Yeller leaves a pup, however, and to such a dog *Savage Sam,* the third of the trilogy, is dedicated. Metaphors of *Bildung,* or growth, these dogs bridge Gipson's gap between worlds that were and might have been. The publication in 1962 of *Savage Sam* concluded a fictional triad through which Gipson hoped once and for all to be heard, his choice of audience having become part of his message in these years of mental anguish and seriously declining health.

Gipson's *Trail-Driving Rooster* is one of the finest tall tales in Texas literature. Rambunctious and fanciful, the story starts in South Texas but really gets under way a couple of weeks later when the trail drivers reach the Llano River in the Hill Country. A rooster named Dick, half Mexican and half Texan, is the central character, a kind of vernacular mascot for Texans.

> Dick's mama . . . built her nest . . . in the top of a Spanish dagger plant, about five feet off the ground. This was to get it out of reach of all the bobcats, foxes, coyotes, and skunks that infested the brush. The dagger plant grows leaves that resemble swords and have sharper points. . . . any chicken-eating varmint trying to climb to that nest through those blades was "just asking to get stabbed in the goozle!" and Dick's mama knew this. . . . Dick's mama was a "pure-blooded Mexican chicken, smarter than a whip." (Pp. 7–8)

A runt, Dick insists on his place in life, and he is thoroughly uncompromising about his dignity and freedom. A cheat and a trickster, he is also more courageous than a gunman when he fights social injustice. Handicapped, he learns to improvise and adjust: to climb trees before he feathers out enough to fly, to play dead when his situation is unclear, and to fight long enough to win the respect of those who defeat him. Ugly but valiant, he ultimately wins because he is ingenious, loud, and flamboyant. A David to whatever Goliath might threaten the band of Texan trail drivers as they graze their longhorns through the Indian Territory and into rough, tough Dodge City, Dick, the "little red rooster" (p. 75), embodies the folk virtues of the tall Texan myth: he fights cowpunchers, he scatters Indians, and "mounted on a grizzly bear," using "a rattlesnake to keep the pore critter whipped into a dead run" (p. 70), he rides the prairies.

In addition to Dick's character as a Texas mascot, his folk-hero origin stands out in this well-furnished novella. A hybrid of Indian Mexico and American Texas, the bird draws on two traditions, one intuitive and accustomed to dealing with stronger adversaries from a position of weakness, the other idealistic and foolhardy. From the earliest Recollection Creek stories through "*The Cow Killers*", Gipson tried to combine two warring traditions: love of the land's ideal beauty with a sense of its resources and wealth, the unity of The People who possess mystery and religion with the science of *los matavacas.* Gipson's rooster Dick carries selected traits of both heritages. The conjunction of the United States and Mexico in Texas, where Gipson saw the two traditions meeting, became increasingly important to him after he finished this triad of novels.

The Trail-Driving Rooster takes place largely over expanses of "high, rolling prairies . . . before white man, in his ignorance and greed, had had time to destroy one of the greatest grass-growing countries on the face of the earth" (p. 34). *Old Yeller,* on the other hand, the novel that "had a sort of double meaning," is set some fifteen years earlier in "a new country and a good one" with "plenty of grass, wood, and water, . . . wild game for the killing" and "fertile ground for growing bread corn."[8] The time of the novel is that of Gipson's parents' births, just after the Civil War. The Mason area was then a developing frontier, and most settlers would have been in this part of the Hill Country only two or three years. The earliest Germans, who would then have been there about a decade, were the old families. In Mason the two important changes following the end of the Civil War were the conclusion of the vicious *Henkerzeit,* a nativistic backlash when vigilante units of roving Confederates swept the countryside executing or conscripting Unionist German and American settlers along the remote frontier, and the "return of U.S. soldiers to the Texas forts" (p. 2) like Fort Mason to restore order and recontain the Indians. During these years, the Indian depredations were concluding as the cattle drives up the Western Trail were starting. The setting of *Old Yeller,* the most popular Texas novel, includes these historical elements.[9]

The action starts with a cattle drive: "Papa and a bunch of other Salt Licks settlers formed a 'pool herd' of their little separate bunches of steers and trailed them to the new market—at Abilene, Kansas. This was to get 'cash money,' which most Texans needed just after the Civil War" (pp. 1–2). The character central to the reader's view of this Anglo-American settlement is young Travis Coates. Looking back on these times, much as Hopper Creech remembers that special year along Recollection Creek, Travis recalls the men preparing to leave: "They told their folks what to do in case the Indians came off the reservation or the coons got to eating the corn or the bears got to killing too many hogs. Then they gathered their cattle, burned a trail brand on their hips, pulled out on the long trail to Kansas" (pp. 2–3).

Recalling the story in the practiced conventions of oral narration, Travis continues,

> I remember how it was the day Papa left. . . . And I remember how Mama was trying to keep from crying. . . .
>
> I wasn't about to cry. I was fourteen years old, pretty near a grown man. . . . Papa reached down and put a hand on my shoulder.
>
> "Now Travis," he said "you're getting to be a big boy; and while I'm gone, you'll be the man of the family." (P. 3)

The older Travis Coates telling this story thus remembers his way back into the character of a fourteen-year-old growing up in the frontier Salt Licks settlement that embraces Birdsong Creek and the Coates family's home.

> Mama had named [the creek] when she and Papa came to settle. She said she named it the first day she and Papa got there, with Mama driving the ox cart . . . and with Papa driving the cows and horses. They'd meant to build closer to the other settlers, over on

> Salt Branch. But they'd camped there at the spring, and the bee myrtle had been blooming white that day, and seemed like in every bush there was a mockingbird, singing his fool head off. It was all so pretty and smelled so good and the singing birds made such fine music that Mama wouldn't go on.
>
> "We'll build right here," she'd told Papa.
>
> And that's what they'd done. Built themselves a home right here on Birdsong Creek and fought off the Indians and cleared a corn patch and raised me and Little Arliss and lost a little sister who died of a fever.
>
> Now it was my home, too. And while Papa was gone, it was up to me to look after it. (P. 7)

By the time the family acquires the stray yellow dog with one ear chewed off, Travis has told how the double-pen log cabin was built and chinked, how the dog run is "a good place to eat watermelons in the hot summer" (p. 9), and how he does the daily chores in this world where families are the unit of survival.

When Old Yeller comes into the novel, the world of Birdsong Creek is complete. The two-room cabin of the Coates family houses a dog now in addition to Travis's mother and his younger brother Arliss. A whole network of similarly fatherless homes extends throughout the Salt Licks community. One shiftless old man, cast from the mold of Restless Solomon in *Recollection Creek*, stays behind to look after the women, but the only assurance this old Buddy Searcy really brings is to drift in just before noon, eat a heavy dinner, and rest in the shade of the dog run until suppertime, after which he rides back home, pleased with himself and content in his role. Though inconsequential most of the time, he can fulfill important needs, should problems befall the settlement, precisely because he is redundant. His eleven-year-old granddaughter Lizbeth befriends Travis and reminds him of his dead sister.[10]

As children in the novel mirror the adult world, so too do

animals, domestic and wild, extend the human world. The traits and functions assigned to animals reflect the order that humans create, and disruptions in the animal kingdom parallel aberrations in human order. Young Travis Coates knows that nature is tough to control, and during his father's absence Travis recognizes that his duty is to maintain order. Only at the end of the novel, if then, does he learn much about the lesson his mother gives him early in the novel. When Old Yeller strays to the Coates home and steals "the only meat . . . left from last winter's hog butchering" (p. 14), young Travis sees him as "a big ugly slick-haired yeller dog" with "one short ear . . . chewed clear off and his tail . . . bobbed so close to his rump that there was hardly stub enough left to wag" (p. 13), but his mother says, "'Well, Travis, . . . it looks like we've got us a dog, . . . and you'll have to admit he's a smart dog. Mighty few dogs have sense enough to figure out a way to reach a side of meat hanging that high. He must have climbed up on top of that meat barrel and jumped from there'" (p. 16). Later, the dog's intelligence serves the family well when he warns them of dangers and threats of death. Without him, they might not have survived.

Gradually Old Yeller wins Travis's affection when he saves the younger brother, Little Arliss, from an angry bear trying to rescue her cub from Arliss. Travis's account of the incident is one of Gipson's most vivid and tense passages:

> . . . the she bear was charging across the shallows in the creek. She was knocking sheets of water high in the bright sun, charging with her fur up and her long teeth bared, filling the canyon with that awful coughing roar. And no matter how fast Mama ran or how fast I ran, the she bear was going to get there first!
>
> I think I nearly went blind then, picturing what was going to happen to Little Arliss. I know that I opened my mouth to scream and not any sound came out.
>
> Then, just as the bear went lunging up the creek bank toward

Little Arliss and her cub, a flash of yellow came streaking out of the brush.

It was that big yeller dog. He was roaring like a mad bull. He wasn't one-third as big and heavy as the she bear, but when he piled into her from one side, he rolled her clear off her feet. They went down in a wild, roaring tangle of twisting bodies and scrambling feet and slashing fangs.

As I raced past them, I saw the bear lunge up to stand on her hind feet like a man while she clawed at the body of the yeller dog hanging to her throat. I didn't wait to see more. Without ever checking my stride, I ran in and jerked Little Arliss loose from the cub. I grabbed him by the wrist and yanked him up out of that water and slung him toward Mama like he was a half-empty sack of corn. I screamed at Mama. "Grab him, Mama! Grab him and run!" Then I swung my chopping axe high and wheeled, aiming to cave in the she bear's head with the first lick.

But I never did strike. I didn't need to. Old Yeller hadn't let the bear get close enough. He couldn't handle her; she was too big and strong for that. She'd stand there on her hind feet, hunched over, and take a roaring swing at him with one of those big front claws. She'd slap him head over heels. She'd knock him so far that it didn't look like he could possibly get back there before she charged again, but he always did. He'd hit the ground rolling, yelling his head off with the pain of the blow; but somehow he'd always roll to his feet. And here he'd come again, ready to tie into her for another round.

I stood there with my axe raised, watching them for a long moment. Then from up toward the house, I heard Mama calling; "Come away from there, Travis. Hurry, son! Run!"

That spooked me. Up till then, I'd been ready to tie into that bear myself. Now suddenly, I was scared out of my wits again. I ran toward the cabin.

But like it was, Old Yeller nearly beat me there. I didn't see it, of course; but Mama said that the minute Old Yeller saw we were all in the clear and out of danger, he threw the fight to that she

> bear and lit out for the house. The bear chased him for a little piece, but at the rate Old Yeller was leaving her behind, Mama said it looked like the bear was backing up.
>
> But if the big yeller dog was scared or hurt in any way when he came dashing into the house, he didn't show it. He sure didn't show it like we all did. (Pp. 48–53)

Later the dog trees a wild turkey gobbler for Travis, guards the corn patch, breaks a young cow for milking, and eventually saves Travis from angry hogs.

> Old Yeller . . . saved me. Just like he'd saved Little Arliss. . . . He came in, roaring with rage. He flung himself between me and the killer hogs. Fangs bared, he met them head on, slashing and snarling. He yelled with pain as the savage tushes ripped into him. . . . He gave me that one-in-a-hundred chance to get free. (P. 105)

Though the boy is seriously injured and his dog is mauled, Travis gets Old Yeller and himself back to the cabin, which seems miles away.

During the weeks while he and the dog are recuperating, Bud Searcy's granddaughter Lizbeth stays with the Coates family, becoming the daughter that the family had lost. Without Lizbeth's help, corn could not have been picked, the cows milked, or the garden gathered. During this time, an incipient rabies epidemic that old Searcy and a newcomer rancher had heard about afflicts the Coates cattle, including their bull and their new milch cow. Travis shoots the bull, and the family hauls wood to burn the carcass, thinking to slow the contagion. The stench is so bad during the burning of the bull that they wait to shoot the cow until after she has rambled some distance away from the cabin.

Mrs. Coates and Lizbeth, guarded by Old Yeller, spend a whole summer day burning the cow. As they ride home on their mule Juniper, they stop at the creek to drink and narrowly miss being attacked by a gray wolf, "big and savage enough to hamstring a horse or drag down a full-grown cow" (p. 147). Old Yeller, "weak and crippled" (p. 147), keeps the wolf "slowed down" as the two women escape on the mule. "'It's sure a good thing that Old Yeller was along to keep him fought off,'" Travis acknowledges. "Mama waited a little bit, then said in a quiet voice: 'It was a good thing for us, son, but it wasn't good for Old Yeller'" (p. 151). Travis has, until now, never doubted the dog's ability to recover.

> Then it hit me what Mama was getting at. All my insides froze. I couldn't get my breath.
>
> I jumped to my feet, wild with hurt and scare. "But Mama!" I cried out. "Old Yeller's just saved your life! He's saved my life. He's saved Little Arliss's life." (P. 152)

Firm in her sure knowledge of nature—"'it would be you or me or Little Arliss or Lizbeth next'" (p. 152)—Mrs. Coates leads Travis to his necessary conclusion that the dog which has repeatedly saved them has been infected with rabies and now must be shot. "'We've got to do it,'" she tells Travis. "'We just can't take the chance'" (p. 152).

Days later, with the crops harvested, fences repaired, and the epidemic having subsided, Travis's father returns from Kansas with the horse that Travis had wanted.

> "That was rough," he tells his son. "That was as rough a thing as I ever heard tell of happening to a boy. . . . You couldn't ask any more of a grown man. . . . It's not a thing you can forget. I don't guess it's a thing that you ought to forget." (P. 156)

"'What I mean is,'" the father concludes, as Gipson's spokesman, "'things like that happen. They may seem might cruel and unfair, but that's how life is a part of the time. But that isn't the only way life is. A part of the time, it's mighty good. And a man can't afford to waste all the good part, worrying about the bad parts'" (p. 156).

Nowhere else does Gipson state the purpose of his juveniles more pointedly, vindicating himself too of charges that his writings for children were unduly violent. And nowhere else is the shortcoming that ultimately triggered his own destruction more clear. Gipson's solution for encountering life, the struggle to balance the "cruel and unfair" parts with the "good parts," is a little more of the ongoing Gipson autobiography, written before it became apparent.

Yet, the book concludes with what seems a strong affirmation of faith in renewal and regeneration. Old Yeller leaves a pup that becomes Savage Sam. Little Arliss grows into Travis's role. Travis henceforth will train his young brother and the new dog, but Travis himself has become a horseman, the next thing to being a grown man.

Old Yeller deserves its fame as a children's novel of *Bildung*, or growth. But within the context of Gipson's other writings, the novel assumes mythic, and ominous, proportions. Affinities between *Old Yeller* and *Fabulous Empire*, the Col. Zack Miller biography that became a kind of self-fulfilling prophecy of Gipson's life, are particularly resonant. Miller's most formidable enemies are time and luck; for him progress means holding his own for as long as possible. When one does get ahead, because occasionally good luck comes, the gains are to be marshaled as a reserve against ever more devastating onslaughts of time, which ravishes both places and people. Finally, though, one runs out of luck and out of reserves and may be forced to sacrifice something precious—probably the very possession he has tried to preserve, the thing that has preserved him.

Old Yeller clarifies and simplifies life, preparing young people for loss and violence. The dog drops into the life of this needful and worthy frontier family, much as does Lizbeth Searcy, and in the end, must be shot by the people the dog has lived to defend. But the dog gives Travis Coates a "one-in-a-hundred chance" to make it.

Much as the dog functions in the novel, *Old Yeller* is a vehicle to move others a little closer to the "final Utopia." Yet the death of the dog, however plausible the circumstances, augurs despondingly for Gipson. Old Yeller is a product of the same period during which Gipson created Aaron Blood, Gipson's dark voice in *Recollection Creek* and the only strikingly original emendation Gipson made while fashioning the stories of *Recollection Creek* into a novel. The hermit of the novel in which Gipson reveals himself so naively becomes the old yellow dog of *Old Yeller.* Other reciprocities, especially of tone, exist between the two novels, but none so striking as the sense one has that *Old Yeller* answers *Recollection Creek* and that the dog sums up Aaron Blood. While Aaron Blood offers Hopper and Jay a fleeting moment of freedom on their way to manhood with his gift of horses, Old Yeller gives Travis Coates only a chance for survival. Travis will have to do the rest, his father explains to him, on his own. This message follows Gipson's purpose that young people needed to be taught about violence, not protected from it—an explanation he gave after critics commented on violence in his juveniles. Yet Gipson himself spoke gruffly about *Old Yeller,* perhaps because it pointed so clearly toward loss and closure. For one knows from the context of Gipson's writings that the longer Travis Coates lives, the greater his likelihood of someday not being able to balance the "bad" with the "good." Most readers are troubled by the disconcerting imagery associated with Aaron Blood, whom Gipson increasingly resembles during his years of psychological and physical decline from 1957 until his death, but all in all, the imagery of *Old Yeller* teaches a darker lesson.[11]

One may surmise with more assurance about *Old Yeller* than

about Gipson's other works, with the possible exception of *The Trail-Driving Rooster,* that the novel conveys both private and public meaning. Its significance for Gipson in no way detracted from but rather enhanced its meaning for the millions who bought the novel in the United States and abroad and saw the movie, even though the Disney movie telescopes the action of the novel so that much of the book's deeper meaning and Gipson's verisimilitude are lost. For an author who preferred Russell to Remington because Russell's depictions of movements were more accurate, Gipson winced as he wrote the screenplay.[12] Assisted by William Tunberg, he did eventually prepare a script that gave the public a spectacle of catharsis—moving actions set against memorable scenes offering images of meaning.[13]

Savage Sam, published in 1962 after several years during which Gipson's weakening health permitted him to do little writing, was intended as a sequel to *Old Yeller* and possesses considerable merit. Based on the popular Hill Country story of Herman Lehmann, a German youngster captured by Apaches on his parents' farm near Mason in 1870,[14] *Savage Sam* is Gipson's final attempt to paint the "Big Adventure" of childhood.[15] His last major novel, *Savage Sam* was the first book for which Gipson remembered his impetus to write. His "field work," though it left him with impressions still vivid nearly fifty years later, ironically almost cost Gipson his life. In 1915, as a seven-year-old, Gipson traveled with his family to the small settlement of Katemcy to watch Lehmann, then fifty-five, perform feats of endurance and bravery, culminating in the ceremonial killing of a range steer, in lieu of a buffalo. As young Gipson prepared to watch Lehmann perform the kill, the steer headed straight toward Gipson, Lehmann following directly behind. The old German's arrow passed through the steer's body and narrowly missed Gipson's head. Stunned by the near mishap, Gipson and the crowd watched in horror as Lehmann leaped from his horse, cut the liver out, and ate it raw only a few feet before their eyes. Gipson's recollection of that sultry day, in particular, with its smells of dust, sweat, and blood, and of many other burning days in the Southwest, when sounds and smells blur into one intense and violent impression, sustains the imagery of *Savage Sam.* Picaresque, exciting, and colorful, this novel outperforms the more classical and monochromatic *Old Yeller,* though it never surpasses the warmth and dignity of *Old Yeller;* but as a movie sequel, released in 1963, *Savage Sam* "was one Disney that really didn't pay off."[16]

The novel begins cinematically with the dog, Savage Sam—son of Old Yeller, "the worst thief, the biggest glutton, the fiercest fighter, and the greatest old fraud" of the Hill Country (p. 12)—but the view quickly rises and widens to embrace the lay of the land in the 1870s.

> Our part of Texas was a rough country of brushy hogback ridges and rock-bench slopes, with wide mesquite flats and deep-cut canyons and tight little valleys studded with great gnarled live oaks. Willows, pecans, elms, and cottonwoods lined the watercourses.
>
> It was also a country where the weather was generally too hot or too cold, too wet or too dry. But this year had been one of the rare ones . . . so that now the bluestem grass covered the ground like the shaggy pelt of some huge animal . . . tall and green as a wheat field, clear to the tops of the highest ridges. The hot sunlight put a glimmer and sheen on the blades as they bowed before the running wind waves.
>
> Ripe prickly-pear apples shone red through the tossing grass. Cenizo bloomed lavender. And snow-white against the green of the grass drooped long, top-heavy sprays of flowering bee myrtle, filling the air with their sharp, clean fragrance. (P. 10)

In this pellucid setting with its unattenuated colors, young Travis and Arliss Coates and Lizbeth Searcy recall what the frontier was like a decade earlier. The eyes of the two younger ones widen with excitement as sixteen-year-old Travis, only somewhat older than the others, narrates scenes from his first year there. Lost in their reveries the children ride afield, up narrowing canyons and draws, following the dog's trailing barks to a cave where Sam has holed a bobcat. Caught up in the excitement of disengaging themselves and the dog from the vicious cat, they do not hear the approach of an Indian raiding party. Captured within moments, the three children are tied to horses the Indians have just stolen, and the party rides quickly away, Savage Sam in loud pursuit of his young wards.

Gipson's tale, up to this point closely following the experiences of Herman Lehmann and his siblings, focuses on the two most dramatic and visual aspects of the captive narrative tradition: the abduction and pursuit. For days, the "faint, far-carrying trail cry" (pp. 60–61) of Savage Sam following them, the children resist their captors and endure cruel punishments, until finally Travis escapes during a skirmish with troops. Sunburned and without clothes or shoes, he strips a dead soldier and joins the dog in pursuit. Eventually a recovery party of local militia, Travis's father included, overtakes him and the dog. Nine men and eight horses now, they follow the Indian raiders "across a rolling sea of grass so vast that it seemed to have no beginning and no end, moving under a spread of sky that stretched out beyond any distance a body could bring himself to believe" (p. 134).

As the group camps at night, Travis remains puzzled by something that had first occurred to him days before with the Indians, who, though fierce, seemed to Travis childlike in curiosity and awe. He also hears his father and his father's friend, Burn Sanderson,[17] talk about the Indians in much the same way, combining understanding with determination to win nonetheless. For father Coates and Burn Sanderson, the Indians "had a better right to the country . . . than the white man" (p. 143). As Travis was confused by the Indians, both childlike and vicious, so is he also confused by these white adults who could kill Indians—and kill them he knew they would—and still recognize their preeminent rights.

The defeat of these Indians and the safe return of Lizbeth, whose possible sexual abuse has concerned the older whites, and the recovery of scrappy Little Arliss would be anticlimactic in comparison with Travis's epiphany of understanding were Gipson not a masterful raconteur. The final battle wages intensely, with Travis himself involved, but at various points the sounds and smells of the battlefield subside as the action goes into slow motion, and Travis feels left in the solitude of his thoughts. He learns that "man is never far from his primitive origins."[18] He sees

> how close life is tied up with death, so that you can't have one without the other. Everything on earth kills to live, then turns around and gets killed, so that something else can live. That was the pattern. I could see it now; and I guessed there wasn't a thing, from a man to a tumblebug, could change it. . . .
>
> Maybe me and Lizbeth and Little Arliss and Papa and Mama and friends of ours, like Burn Sanderson, didn't amount to any more in this world than any other living creature. But like all other creatures . . . our lives were important to us, and each of us would fight to keep them just as long as we could—and try to help those we loved to do the same. (P. 146)

As Travis looks down into the face of a badly wounded Indian—"no fear in those black eyes, and no hate—just intense curiosity" (p. 202)—the young boy, almost a man, recognizes that what he "wanted most of all was to bridge the wide gap" that lay between the Indian's way of thinking and his own (p. 203). Most of *Recollection Creek* is narrated as a daydream vision, as are memorable passages in *Fabulous Empire, The Home Place,* and *Old Yeller.* A technique Gipson often uses for conclusion, the vision is, however, nowhere else in Gipson's writings handled in such close conjunction with the events surrounding the dream. As the battle ebbs and flows, so Travis's thoughts wage until both dream and battle conclude with force in the last line of the novel.

A highly personalized novel based on a story that appeals powerfully to the Hill Country imagination, *Savage Sam* concludes Gipson's development as a writer. Written from a single episode, the novel achieves complete unity, in contrast with the episodic plots of Gipson's earlier novels and biographies. The imagery assumes almost a painterly, up-front quality, with landscapes pressing into the foreground and horizons dropping out of sight. Gipson's colors here are more varied but flatter than in his earlier work. Perspectives change frequently and dramatically, Gipson having learned how to narrow the view to a telling gesture and then let the narrative roll again. And above all, he unites interior and exterior action, looking into things while at the same time seeing them. Previously Gipson used the device of an older narrator observing himself at a younger age in order to "doubly paint" the soul, as it was and is now in the narrative present.[19] His technique in *Savage Sam* is subtler: while telling the story in first person, Gipson invests Travis Coates with a kind of double vision.[20]

While Gipson's concentration of plot in *Savage Sam* does not quite surpass the overall unity of effect he achieved in *Old Yeller,*[21] the movie version of *Savage Sam,* Gipson's fourth movie, which premiered in Mason in 1963, never achieved the success of the *Old Yeller* movie. Criticized as clichéd and overdirected, the production was especially faulted for inconsistency with Gipson's tone.[22] Though financially successful, Disney's *Savage Sam* failed to communicate much of Gipson's design. Gipson himself suffered acutely while he wrote and rewrote the script. His alcoholism had worsened, he was frequently incapacitated by rages, and his personal life had disintegrated. Rumors circulated in Mason about his condition.[23] But no one, other than perhaps Gipson himself in *Old Yeller,* foresaw an event of 1962 that triggered a death in the Gipson family and darkened the father's life.

On Thursday, June 14, 1962, the older son Mike Gipson, a student and an aspiring writer, returned home from the University of Texas, frustrated with his work. The family had recently moved to the more prosperous and attractive "German" part of the county, the part from which a young Fred Gipson had felt excluded, to a "ranch" homesteaded by an old German family named Reichenau, a surname that Gipson knew translated as "rich valley." After reaching home, Mike Gipson drove back to Mason with his younger brother Beck. When Mike and Beck returned, Mike found his dog, the prototype of Savage Sam, chained and clubbed to death in a shed behind the new family home overlooking the Llano River. In shock, Mike drove back to Austin and ended his life that weekend, on a Father's Day that coincided that year with his brother Beck's birthday.[24] Ever concerned for this sensitive son, so like Gipson himself in the seemingly prescient description of Steve Crockett in *The Home Place,* Fred Gipson saw the drying up of "Recollection Creek," his name for the new home.[25]

The death of Mike Gipson, whatever its complex causes, and whatever transpired in the gaps between the sequence of events just presented, signaled the end of the dream as surely as the death of Old Yeller in the novel foreboded the author's end. The rest of Gipson's life would go to searching for whatever dream would take him, as Col. Zack Miller had once hoped, to another frontier where he could "get a start in a new country."[26] When Tommie Gipson left in August, 1963, a month after the premiere of *Savage Sam,* and divorced Gipson in 1964, the collapse that had started in the late 1950s was complete. Within weeks, the old Gipson house on the other side of Mason at the old Gooch place, the land where Gipson had grown up and where he and his wife reared their children, went up in flames one Sunday morning. Gipson was the only witness to this further loss. Then his mother and Webb and Dobie died. As Gipson had written in *Fabulous Empire,* "it was back off and start over, with nothing but his two bare hands, or tuck his tail and admit that he was done for good."[27] Yet his search took the form of retreat: to the back roads and wilds of Texas and the Southwest and Mexico, always looking for a perfect valley and a perfect woman so he could write. But Gipson never published a major work again during his lifetime. The two posthumous publications, *Little Arliss* and *Curly and the Wild Boar,* warrant attention mainly as improvisations on the subject of delinquency. Although Gipson may have intended to publish them separately, he probably planned to join them eventually, as he characteristically did, with other stories to build a longer novel. But the ability to sustain such writing was gone, though the will to write never left him during the last ten lonesome years while he sought renewal and peace.[28]

CHAPTER SEVEN

"Peace Is a Dream" 1965–1973

To the extent that the Southwest perceives itself as an alter ego of mainstream America, the myth that informs Fred Gipson's writing should not be interpreted as nostalgia alone, but rather as an attempt by a community of believers to survive in the shadow of a dominant culture, as has Appalachia, from which many Hill Country Anglos were drawn. The structures that undergird Gipson's fiction and histories and the relationships of works, author, and audience reveal a hierarchy of values and a social construction of reality communicated through compelling metaphors and symbols.[1] In his writings for young people, Gipson's purpose shows most clearly. Working back from *Savage Sam, Old Yeller,* and *The Trail-Driving Rooster* to *"The Cow Killers", The Home Place, Hound-Dog Man, Fabulous Empire,* and *Recollection Creek* affords widening glimpses of the dream that lit Gipson's soul, reflecting a world gone by onto one coming. For in his earlier works, Gipson's glance shifted, and though it ranged over wider surfaces, it was never as direct as in the children's books, his most future-oriented retrospectives.

Cornelia Meigs has long since identified the common source of children's and national literatures:

> in the vast collection of dear familiar stories told around the cottage fires in humble houses or in the great poetic narratives recited or sung in the halls of palace and castle. . . . In that ancient world . . . there was little distinction between what entertained the elders and what entertained the young. . . . There is a power and life in those stories which have penetrated through every superimposed layer of time, through conquest and growth and Christian conversion. . . . We see, in these stories of immense age, above everything else man's effort to explain to himself the forces of which he was so vaguely and reverently aware in the material and spiritual world around him, to explain them without the help of science or the illumination of revealed religion.[2]

Gipson's later works make more explicit the purpose at which the earlier works hinted. The worldview that manifests itself in this literature is the product of a residual, intuitive America where assimilation has been slow, neither just escapist nor just reversionary but projecting an America that was and, in the regional idiom, "might ought" to have been. This literature is characteristic of the fiction and history that emerging nations produce: mythopoetic, vernacular in setting and form, and affective in that it reifies the body politic.

Gipson's works reveal the author's consistent orientation to setting, the ever-changing union and disunion of place and time—terrain and memory—as a highly personalized world invested with meaning and precedent. This union evoked poetic descriptions of a world as seen through bifocal vision—realistic foregrounds, romantic horizons—the landscape giving a sense of centrality or order. But the tension of disunion through change or forgetting threatened Gipson's world. The more he extended himself into that lost world, feeling that he could no longer be himself apart from it and hardly able to distinguish between himself and it, the more his own existence was threatened. Gipson suffered acutely during the drought of the 1950s, his own declining health reflecting the illnesses of his land. As the only place where he could be himself was shrinking, Gipson saw his own possibilities circumscribed. The books of his productive 1950s, along with *Savage Sam* in 1962, were a last flowering, Gipson's way of doing battle much as desert plants seed rapidly after a rain.

Early in the 1960s, Gipson built and named "Recollection Creek," a farm since then styled a "ranch," siting his home on a high place above the Llano River where the bluffs narrow before widening into a valley dropping toward the east.[3] The sun rose there over a shaded terrace climbing from the river up to the house, and it set beyond a high plateau that rose toward Blue Mountain, its last rays running the river gold. Hunkered down to the ground at the edge of a tree line, ventilated by seasonal breezes, the house was Gipson's retreat, like his stories, where he could build a world on his own terms—rising early, sleeping during the heat of day, watching the stars at night, with a big fireplace and surrounded by all the symbols of youth, but ultimately alone: "Because, from the very beginning, you ignored one thing—the human element."[4]

Gipson's novel, *The Home Place,* in which this "human element" surfaces as the great dream killer, took a fortunate turn at the end and the Crockett family survived despite the "human element" and secured its future at the price of retreat to a sequestered valley. But Gipson's life fifteen years later was not so ideally constructed. Having turned his sights in the 1950s toward children, hoping to reach them before they went wrong, he stumbled now toward his own salvation, cognizant that his days of empire-building were over and that his life would close if he could not reach a new frontier.

The home at "Recollection Creek" was symbolic of Gipson's values in the same way that his writings once had been, and now his search for cures in the indigenous culture of his region was symptomatic of his illness.[5] Such cures, older than the Anglos and older even than the Germans in the Southwest, he hoped the Mexicans would reveal to him from their ancestors, the Indians, whom Gipson believed he understood, having found their artifacts as a boy and learning as a man the secret ways people close to the earth have of speaking through metaphors and symbols that the Indians called the "Inside Song."[6]

To a degree, his writings had already reflected this inclination toward the vernacular and indigenous—a kind of "region, roots, and race" imperative that colored American literature and history in the 1950s and 1960s, and from which Texas writing only reluctantly budges.[7] Later in the 1960s, while the current of American thought shifted to re-examination of the saga of America, Gipson continued to dig deeper in directions from which the nation as a whole had turned. The art he knew and liked fell from favor, but he repeatedly attempted to find shortcuts to the experienced and intuitive wisdom from which he believed such art sprang.[8] He traveled the wilds of Texas and Mexico, looking for the soul and wife that eluded him, and he drove to New Mexico on assignment for the *New York Times* to interview Peter Hurd shortly after Hurd's portrait of Lyndon Johnson had aroused the presidential ire of Gipson's contemporary from across the Hill Country.[9]

In the mountains at San Patricio, Gipson and Hurd reflected on the absent Lyndon Johnson, and in so doing, they reflected on the precarious coherence of their own lives and region. The three of them—Gipson, Hurd, and Johnson—represented the democratic thrust of grassroots regionalism: tributes of the current to their source, fervently trying to use the past to communicate with the present. About all three one might have wondered, as a biographer did about Johnson, how a style and a purpose "so suitable for the world of the fifties" could become "so faltering in the 1960s – the world of television, civil wars in Asia, and a civil rights movement at home?"[10]

Loss and its incumbent anxiety troubled Johnson and Gipson, particularly in their final years as both sought their own versions of the ideal America. The more they felt their intent to communicate thwarted, the more they became radicalized. As Edward Ruhe suggests, "If the malaise of the pastoralist is a form of alienation, the drive that makes primitivism seem inviting may be a radical form of that malaise."[11]

Falls from grace are hardly more conclusive in politics than they are in literary criticism. Johnson grieved about how the future would rank him, and Gipson worried that the future would get along without knowing the things he knew. "'Who is going to tell the tales now?'" muses latter-day Hill Country writer Elroy Bode on the passing of the old generation in *This Favored Place.* "'Who will tell the young ones of the traditions?' And it was true . . . that the old men who talked at night in the front-porch swings and who handed on the family heritage to whoever would listen – they had passed now. And there was not anyone left to take their place; their century was finally over."[12] Despite dropping sales, Gipson's *Old Yeller, Savage Sam, Hound-Dog Man, Cowhand, "The Cow Killers", Little Arliss,* and *Curly and the Wild Boar* have remained in print since his death in 1973, and John Graves acknowledges that, however one judges the quality of Gipson's work, Gipson "has probably been . . . the most widely read and appreciated writer Texas has ever produced."[13]

Especially mutable is the fate of any writer who takes root in a particular style of living rather than in living itself. While the cause enjoys popularity, the books will be read for partisan reasons. When opinion shifts, those books will seldom be read at all without some wincing and embarrassment. Yet to Gipson's credit, he remained remarkably consistent, probably too consistent, in his development while critical taste changed all around him. Today the myth of the country seems once again merging with Gipson's world as a warmer, more organic ethic again romanticizes particularism, the vernacular, and the small town—and the West and the Southwest as the "new moral frontier" of America.[14]

More than popularity, however, is at stake in assessing Gipson because Gipson's metaphors range the culture. If his fiction and history—and there is little essential difference between his handling of these genres—reflect a heritage of idealism, youthfulness, and purpose, the writings also reveal closure, contradiction, and sterility. For good or ill, the progression of metaphors in Gipson's writing reflects the counterpoint of American civilization. Gipson mourned with Yaquis and Apaches and Comanches when they saw that "peace is a dream" soon lost, while at the same time he pursued his own dreams of wealth and purity. Attached to the land and caught in a dichotomy of flux, he observed changes of power and status, kinship and culture, that far transcended the narrow Texas heritage recorded by Dobie and Webb. For Gipson wrote of a resurgent consciousness—traditional, visionary, episodic, picaresque, and pastoral—in which literature was a "kind of speculative history, perhaps a superhistory," and history became a "kind of fiction in which we live and hope to survive."[15]

Afterword

Implicit in this volume has been an interest in the writings of one Texas author as they relate to the national culture. Gipson's works suggest that culture is both memory and aspiration, that tradition is both backward-looking *and* forward-looking. But his works do not imply that the person, the family, or the community balances the imperatives of the present easily. Often his works show that survival is best assured by a plurality of options, such as the composite traits of a group rather than the virtuoso efforts of the individual. While Gipson's works reveal the wellsprings of any national literature, they also particularize the imperfect transition of American values from traditional or sacred to secular, and from vernacular to modern and national. Texas has always been a colony of America. The old Texas heritage of radicalism and imperialism turned in the twentieth century into a literature of reaction and escape. The early literature, written by colonists such as Charles Sealsfield, served a national design. The middle literature, to which Gipson's works belong, was written by descendants of colonists. The early ones were escaping from stasis, the later ones from change, the variable being not in the essence but in the context—a variable of time, of what Germans call the *Zeitgeist.* The constants are alienation, escape, and subgrouping. Long subsumed by the South and then eclipsed by the new West of Dobie, Webb, and Zane Grey, nationalistic at heart but colonial in mind, not sure whether to declare independence or to join the commonwealth, more a magical kingdom of raw resources than a legitimate member of the First World (or of the Third World, for that matter), Texas literature is a middle-aged kid seeking identity, trying to grow up, not sure how or whether it wants to. Gipson's work seems to be a part that helps to explain the whole.

Notes

PREFACE

1. Leon Edel, "The Figure under the Carpet," *Telling Lives: The Biographer's Art*, ed. Marc Pachter (1979; rpt. Philadelphia: University of Pennsylvania Press, 1981), pp. 17–34. The thesis of Edel's work is that biographical "subjects stand revealed . . . in the works they wrought, the acts they performed, the shape they gave to their existence" (p. 34).

2. A. C. Greene, *The Fifty Best Books on Texas* (Dallas: Pressworks, 1982), p. 13; Sam H. Henderson, *Fred Gipson*, Southwest Writers Series no. 10, ed. James Ward Lee (Austin: Steck-Vaughn, 1967), pp. 49–50. See also Henderson's unsigned entry on Frederick Benjamin Gipson in *The Handbook of Texas: A Supplement*, vol. 3, ed. Eldon Stephen Branda (Austin: Texas State Historical Association, 1976), pp. 339–40.

3. Tom Lea, in Patrick Bennett, *Talking With Texas Writers: Twelve Interviews* (College Station: Texas University Press, 1980), p. 286.

4. In *Literary Biography* (Toronto: University of Toronto Press, 1957), Leon Edel presents six tenets for literary biographers. I have added another tenet (f) from E. K. Brown's preface to *Willa Cather: A Critical Biography*, completed by Leon Edel (New York: Knopf, 1953), to this list.

a. "A biography is a record, in words, of something that is as mercurial and as flowing, as compact of temperament and emotion, as the human spirit itself. It is what Lytton Strachey once described as 'the most delicate and humane of all branches of the art of writing'" (p. 1).

b. ". . . all biography has this in common, that it is concerned with the truth of life and the truth of experience" (p. 2).

c. Literary biography "is a process: scientific when it asks the sciences to elucidate whatever they can about the human being and his personality; an art when it uses language to capture human experience; and requiring all the craftsmanship an individual can command in mastering and disciplining himself to deal with material as rich and varied and mercurial as the mind of man" (pp. 6–7).

d. "The literary biographer" must at every moment of his task be a critic. His art is an art of "continuing and unceasing criticism" (p. 40).

e. "Certain critics insist that any attempt to relate biography to the artist's work, and in particular any attempt to read the life of the creator in his works constitutes a 'biographical fallacy.' . . . The biographer . . . is inclined to dissent from such a view. He holds *that the personal emotions have not necessarily vanished and that at least a portion of them may be recovered and may perhaps be found to have some relevance*" (p. 51, italics added).

f. A literary biography is written for the "light" an author's "life and character might cast" upon the "art" (p. vii).

g. ". . . at least three main Architectural Ideas [Carlyle, *Sartor Resartus*] can be found in the structure of biographies. . . . The first type of biography might be said to be chronicle; the second pictorial; the third narrative-pictorial or novelistic . . . the biographer's vision of his subject" (pp. 82–83).

CHRONOLOGY

Sources, in order of my dependence upon them, are Mike Cox, *Fred Gipson: Texas Storyteller* (Austin: Shoal Creek, 1980); Stella Gipson Polk, *Mason and Mason County: A History*, rev. ed. (Burnet, Tex.:

Eakin, 1980); Walter Prescott Webb, ed., *The Handbook of Texas,* 2 vols. (Austin: Texas State Historical Association, 1952); Branda, ed., *Handbook of Texas,* vol. 3; and *The Texas Almanac* for various years between 1910 and 1973.

CHAPTER ONE

1. For the history of the German Hill Country community, see Terry G. Jordan, *German Seed in Texas Soil* (Austin: University of Texas Press, 1966); Glen E. Lich and Dona B. Reeves, eds. *German Culture in Texas* (Boston: Twayne, 1980); and Glen E. Lich, "Rural Hill Country: Man, Nature, and the Ecological Perspective," *Eagle in the New World: German Immigration to Texas and America,* ed. Theodore Gish and Richard Spuler (College Station: Texas A&M University Press, for the Texas Committee for the Humanities, 1986), pp. 26–46.

2. Cox, *Fred Gipson,* p. 7, and Polk, *Mason and Mason County,* pp. 117–18. Here and elsewhere, Polk writes colorful and impressionistic sketches of Mason history. She describes early Mason as having "the most evil reputation in Texas for dark deeds" (p. 68), as being a place with mysterious petroglyphs and abundant legends (p. 33), and as a "Promised Land" carved "out of wilderness" (p. 155). This older sister of Fred Gipson says that she often heard such stories as a girl and they held a special kind of wonder (p. 35). What she tells, Fred Gipson later shows in his writings, presumably tapping the same oral tradition that his sister describes vividly throughout her history.

3. Cox, *Fred Gipson,* p. 15.

4. Thomas Beckton ("Beck") Gipson, interview with author, Feb. 5, 1984. Beck Gipson and other informants have spoken of Fred Gipson's love-hate relationship to the land and people. "When he practiced conservation," Gipson said of his father, "he was looking backward. He wanted the land to be what it had been. It was not the kind of conservation most people practiced." Compare, on the subject of the romantic horizon, Robert Rosenblum, *Modern Painting and the Northern*

Romantic Tradition: Friedrich to Rothko (New York: Harper and Row, 1975), p. 197. Farfetched as it might seem, viewing Gipson's writings as somewhere between Friedrich's and Rothko's paintings is instructive, and of course it is possible that Gipson was directly influenced by the Dresden legacy of the Hill Country art of Hermann Lungkwitz and Richard Petri. Katherine Anne Porter's, John Graves's, and Andrew Jolly's writings might similarly be plotted on such a scale.

5. Andrew Jolly, *A Time of Soldiers* (New York: Dutton, 1976), p. 306. Jolly describes an attitude toward place from a tradition in Texas culture that differs significantly from Walter Prescott Webb's and J. Frank Dobie's but which shares aspects with the literature of Gipson and Katherine Anne Porter. Jolly's fiction speaks to many of the values implicit in Gipson's novels and biographies. See Glen E. Lich, "Love on the Rocks: Andrew Jolly's America," *Journal of the American Studies Association of Texas* 14 (1983): 87–95.

6. Frank Wardlaw, quoted in Cox, *Fred Gipson,* p. 208.

7. Beck Gipson, interview, Feb. 5, 1984.

8. Lich, "Animal Metaphors and Verbal Abuse," *T for Texas,* Publications of the Texas Folklore Society no. 45, ed. Francis E. Abernethy (Dallas, Texas: E-Heart, 1982), pp. 177–93. See also Cox, *Fred Gipson.*

9. Cox suggests (*Fred Gipson,* p. 5) and Polk (*Mason and Mason County*) demonstrates the influence of this pervasive oral heritage; Beck Gipson stated (interview, Feb. 5, 1984) that his father preferred to deal with people through stories. Fred Gipson "liked the stories more than he liked the people."

10. Howard Becker, *Through Values to Social Interpretation: Essays on Social Contexts, Actions, Types, and Prospects* (Durham, N.C.: Duke University Press, 1950), pp. 16–17. See also Joe B. Frantz, "Ethnicity and Politics in Texas," in Lich and Reeves, *German Culture in Texas,* pp. 191–202. Mike Cox (interview with author, Feb. 11, 1984), local Mason informants, and Beck Gipson describe Fred Gipson as a remarkable storyteller, schooled by Mason's best raconteurs. His father was, according to Beck Gipson, often preoccupied with the passage of time, a recurrent theme in his stories. See Cox, *Fred Gipson,* pp. 20–24. The Hill Country preserved an extensive oral tradition until well into the

1950s, each town being known for sets of related tales (e.g., the Sheriff Klaerner stories of Fredericksburg and the Herman Lehmann stories of Mason) that were narrated repeatedly in cycles by storytellers recognized as such in the communities. These tales were enriched through variations and performance, since most listeners knew them; besides providing entertainment, they functioned to dramatize local history and to imply values. Such stories were often used as guides to behavior, suggesting that, as with proverbs, one spoke both through the tales and through the medium of the tales. Gipson was not aware of Claude Lévi-Strauss's definition of bricolage (see chap. 4, below), but he grew up observing it in practice. See Lich, "Animal Metaphors and Verbal Abuse."

11. Clause Lévi-Strauss, *The Savage Mind* (Chicago: University of Chicago Press, 1962), pp. 16–22. The structure of family ranking among the Germans and Anglo Americans in the Hill Country has been described by Lich in "Animal Metaphors and Verbal Abuse." A comprehensive treatment of comparable village social hierarchies is Albert Ilien, *Prestige in dörflicher Lebenswelt: Eine explorative Studie* (Tübingen: Ludwig-Uhland-Institut, 1977).

12. Oscar Handlin, *The Uprooted: The Epic Story of the Great Migrations That Made the American People,* 2nd ed. (Boston: Little, Brown, 1973), p. 8.

13. Beck Gipson, interview, Feb. 5, 1984; Cox, *Fred Gipson,* p. 9.

14. Gipson's mentors in hunting and fishing were his father and his father's friend, Charlie Sanders, the prototype for Blackie Scantling in *Hound-Dog Man.*

15. Cox, *Fred Gipson,* pp. 3–4.

16. Beck Gipson, interview, Feb. 5, 1984. See also Cox, *Fred Gipson;* Henderson, *Fred Gipson,* pp. 1–3, 8, 16, 24, 36, 49; and Polk, *Mason and Mason County,* p. 26, where she speaks of the division of Mason County into poor and prosperous parts, and for a discussion of German and Anglo-American mutual hostilities; Cox, *Fred Gipson,* pp. 30–31; Carolyn Cook Gipson (daughter-in-law of Fred Gipson), interview with author, Aug. 15, 1983; Cox, *Fred Gipson,* pp. 2–4, 7–9; also Gilbert J. Jordan, interview with author, Sept. 28, 1983.

17. Cox, *Fred Gipson,* pp. 30–31. Martha Dobie (sister of J. Frank Dobie) of Kerrville informed me, regarding her first cousin Sterling Neville Dobie of Mason, that S. N. Dobie and her brother Frank were very close as young men, having lived and worked and told stories together. Before Gipson went to the University of Texas, he would have known personally of J. Frank Dobie.

18. Fred Gipson, *Before Old Yeller,* ed. C. Richard King (Burnet, Tex.: Eakin, 1980), p. 107.

19. Ibid., p. 114.

CHAPTER TWO

1. Gipson, *Before Old Yeller.*

2. "A Dissertation on 'Coon Hunting" and "New Boots for the Bullfight" reflect these themes more intensely than most of the other longer writings in this anthology. Refer to Edmund Leach, *Culture and Communications: The Logic by Which Symbols Are Connected; An Introduction to the Use of Structural Analysis in Social Anthropology* (Cambridge: Cambridge University Press, 1976), pp. 33–34, 37, 69–70. I am particularly indebted to Leach for his description of anxieties attached to crossing psychic boundaries, for his analysis of ritual condensation through which abstract ideas can be represented, and for his brief comments on "mytho-logic," which I have used freely. My comments on Gipson's early writings also depend on Edel's concept of the biographer's search (Edel, "Figure under the Carpet," pp. 17–34). What Marc Pachter and Justin Kaplan call "the whole sense of the person" and his "personal mythology" (Pachter, ed., *Telling Lives,* p. 13) is vividly drawn in Edel's metaphor of "the figure under the carpet, the evidence in the reverse of a tapestry, the life-myth of a given mask" (pp. 24–25). Each literary author reveals personal codes, Edel states, that a biographer must learn to read (pp. 25, 26).

3. On the use of dialect as subtle social criticism and expression of values, see Robert Pattison, *On Literacy: The Politics of the Word from*

Homer to the Age of Rock (New York: Oxford University Press, 1982), pp. vi–vii, 61–63, 170, 182.

4. Based on a survey of reviews of Gipson's writings, both when first published and, in many cases, when reprinted years later. See Cox, *Fred Gipson,* p. 85.

5. Rudolf Arnheim, "A Plea for Visual Thinking," *The Language of Images,* ed. W. J. T. Mitchell (Chicago: University of Chicago Press, 1980), pp. 171–79. Compare Stella Gipson Polk's advice given many years later to her brother, cited in Cox, *Fred Gipson,* p. 184.

6. Gipson, *Before Old Yeller,* pp. 82–83. All subsequent citations from this volume will be given parenthetically in the text.

7. Cox, *Fred Gipson,* pp. 39–48; King, introduction to *Before Old Yeller.*

8. Robert R. Marett, *Sacraments of Simple Folk,* Gifford Lectures Series (1933; rpt. New York: AMS, 1979).

9. Andrew Jolly, in *A Time of Soldiers,* is particularly hostile toward what he calls the "professional Texan," a term he applied to Webb and Dobie. Gipson's adoption in Austin of the "drugstore cowboy" look was temporary. Only in his language did he retain an exaggerated dialect.

10. See Jim Corder, "Varieties of Ethical Argument, with Some Account of the Significance of *Ethos* in the Teaching of Composition," *Freshman English News* 6, no. 3 (1978): 12–14. See also Leach, *Culture and Communications,* chap. 8. Compare Rosemary Jackson, *Fantasy: The Literature of Subversion* (London: Methuen, 1981), p. 175: "An understanding," Jackson writes, "of the subversion function of fantastic literature emerges from structuralist rather than merely thematic readings of texts." Jackson concludes that as a mode, the fantastic represents "the imagination in exile" and the "real" under scrutiny.

CHAPTER THREE

1. As exemplars of poetic autobiography, William C. Spengemann cites *Sartor Resartus, David Copperfield,* and *The Scarlet Letter.* See Wil-

liam C. Spengemann, *The Forms of Autobiography: Episodes in the History of a Literary Genre* (New Haven, Conn.: Yale University Press, 1980).

2. Edel, *Literary Biography,* p. 40.

3. Fred Gipson, *Recollection Creek* (New York: Harper, 1944–48, 1955), p. 1. All subsequent citations from this edition are given parenthetically in the text.

4. Cox, *Fred Gipson,* pp. 11–12. Herman Lehmann is discussed at greater length in chap. 6, below, as is the episode of the near death of Fred Gipson.

5. Folklorists may divide everyday life and activities into male and female adult spheres. Traditionally in European, American, and some African folklore, a boy remains in the sphere of the mothers until he undergoes initiation into hunting. Correspondingly, the sun, in some mythologies, remains under the tutelage of the moon until able to bear arms. Female and male spheres are not entirely discrete, however, and the transition that takes a boy (or the sun) from one to the other transpires over a period of time.

6. Qualities of Aaron Blood invite speculation. The etymology of the name *Aaron* is particularly interesting in this regard. The Old Testament Aaron, like his brother Moses, was denied entry to the Promised Land. In folklore and mythology, blood signifies covenant and protection. In Texan and Mexican lore, blood and seeds and jewels promise fertility; the three symbols are often combined. Bull's blood is a nearly universal symbol for divination, and the bull itself, as in the Old Testament story of the golden calf, connotes fertility. Horses, such as the ones Aaron Blood gave Hopper and Jay Creech, are archetypal symbols of male freedom. Harnessed (in this case saddled) horses portend good fortune. Gipson's network of signification, more likely acquired through oral transmission and intuition than academically, is fairly consistent with the symbology of Gertrude Jobes, *Dictionary of Mythology, Folklore, and Symbols,* 3 vols. (New York: Scarecrow, 1961).

7. Richard Bauman, "'Any Man Who Keeps More'n One Hound'll Lie to You': Dog Trading and Storytelling at Canton, Texas," *Language in Use: Readings in Sociolinguistics,* ed. John Baugh and Joel Sherzer (Englewood Cliffs, N.J.: Prentice-Hall, 1984), pp. 198–210. See also

Richard Bauman, *Verbal Art as Performance* (Rowley, Mass.: Newburg House, 1977).

8. John Graves, *Hard Scrabble: Observations on a Patch of Land* (New York: Knopf, 1974), pp. 59, 263–67.

9. Fred Gipson, *Fabulous Empire: Colonel Zack Miller's Story* (Boston: Houghton Mifflin, 1946), pp. 5–6. All subsequent citations from this edition will be given parenthetically in the text.

10. See Peter V. Marinelli, *Pastoral* (London: Methuen, 1978), who suggests three major perspectives of the pastoral: a view toward the Golden Age, a reflection on Arcadia and its transformation, and a retreat into childhood. Marinelli does not suggest an organic connectedness in his list of perspectives, but Gipson's life seems a clear progression of someone who started with a recollection of a Golden Age, developed then a sensitivity for Arcadia as a place to be transformed back to what it had been, and who finally retreated into the fiction of childhood.

11. Cox, in *Fred Gipson,* refers on numerous occasions to Gipson's views of the land and includes photographs of Gipson walking his pastures. Beck Gipson (interview with author) says explicitly that his father's conservation plan was restorative rather than adaptive. The dust jackets and back pages of Gipson's books all contain references to Gipson's plans for the land.

12. The best history of Gipson's films—in all there were four with *Savage Sam*—is contained in Cox's biography.

13. Fred Gipson, *Hound-Dog Man* (New York: Harper, 1949), p. 152. All subsequent citations from this edition will be given parenthetically in the text.

14. In some ways, *Hound-Dog Man* softens the rigid and solitary posture in some of the stories of Recollection Creek and in *Fabulous Empire.* Blackie Scantling eventually compromises to secure what he wants; Gipson obviously understood the need for compromise (as his son says, for *forgiveness*), but, his condition worsened by his alcoholism, he refused, or was unable, to do what he knew must be done. As an inhibition will reduce the performance of an otherwise competent speaker, for example, so too Gipson's dependence on alcohol seems

to have aggravated a generally suppressed tendency toward violence and to have impaired his ability to change. Severe allergic reactions trouble several Fred Gipson descendants, according to his daughter-in-law Carolyn Cook Gipson, (interview with author, Apr. 1, 1984). Gipson apparently also suffered allergic reactions to alcohol on occasion.

CHAPTER FOUR

1. Fred Gipson, *The Home Place* (New York: Harper, 1950), p. 1. All subsequent citations from this edition will be given parenthetically in the text.

2. For the rhetorical intention of such a farm novel as *The Home Place,* refer to "Hamlin Garland," *Oxford Companion to American Literature,* 4th ed. (New York: Oxford University Press, 1978). Garland's novels are "characterized by objective realism and ethical romanticism" (p. 306). The parallel to Gipson's "romantic realism" should be striking. See further, regarding the genre of the farm novel: Roy W. Meyer, *The Middle Western Farm Novel in the Twentieth Century* (Lincoln: University of Nebraska Press, 1965), and Gerhard Schweizer, *Bauernroman und Faschismus* (Tübingen: Ludwig-Uhland-Institut, 1976). Meyer presents the farm novelist as historian, arbiter of values, social critic, and psychologist. In varying degrees, and at different times in his life, Gipson appropriated such functions for himself. Schweizer explores the as yet only meagerly studied relationship between folk literature and politics—in Schweizer's case, between the peasant village novel and National Socialism.

3. The parallels include, but are not limited to, dry-land farming, erosion of the land, and tenacity of human culture. Both books are written from the perspective of an intellectual reverted to the life of a "country man," a *Landsmann* or *païsant* who learns to observe, to cope, and to survive. The books make what Graves calls "lasting statements of self."

4. Gilbert J. Jordan, *Yesterday in the Texas Hill Country* (College Station: Texas A&M University Press, 1979), p. 11.

5. Gipson's understanding of other people was thoroughly intuitive and founded in self-knowledge. Time after time, something that Gipson wrote about a historical or fictional character later proved true of Gipson himself. Marc Pachter and several other contributors to *Telling Lives* cite examples of deep-rooted affinities that could explain such correspondence and transfer between biographer and subject. As the biographer necessarily acts upon, or "fictionalizes," the subject, so too, one suspects, the subject influences the biographer. Until he moved to the place called "Recollection Creek" on the Llano River, Gipson showed a recurrent pattern of dissatisfaction with the place and people surrounding him and of longing to be elsewhere. Even after he settled on the Llano in 1961–62, he nurtured a dream of migrating to Mexico where he felt he could get back in touch with the sources of life.

6. See Irwin, *Doubling and Incest,* p. 171. Irwin states that in such situations "'the author's actual self is the one that goes down,' that the writer ends up identifying himself not with what remains but with what is lost, the detached object that is the work." Compare also Gail L. Mortimer, *Faulkner's Rhetoric of Loss: A Study in Perception and Meaning* (Austin: University of Texas Press, 1983).

7. Cox, *Fred Gipson,* pp. 117–18.

8. The tendency to make explicit what is implicit in another work—in this case, another life—is well known to translators and copy painters, as well as to biographers. See Jean Paris, "Translation and Creation," *The Craft and Context of Translation: A Symposium,* ed. William Arrowsmith and Roger Shattuck (Austin: University of Texas Press, 1961), p. 61.

9. Fred Gipson, *Big Bend: A Homesteader's Story,* with J. O. Langford (Austin: University of Texas Press, 1955), p. 4. All subsequent citations from this edition will be given parenthetically in the text. The genre of fantasy, in which the Langford family's quest for a "fantastic country" must initially be placed, has been properly linked in recent scholarship with subversion. Consult Jackson, *Fantasy;* Eric S. Rabkin, *The Fantastic in Literature* (Princeton, N.J.: Princeton University Press,

1973). Fred Gipson was writing a form of fantasy in that he was not simply depicting but also reconstructing his dream world.

10. Alfred Crosby, *The Columbian Exchange: Biological and Cultural Consequences of 1492* (Westport, Conn.: Greenwood, 1972).

11. Cox, *Fred Gipson,* pp. 117–18.

12. Gipson and Boatright were close. Gipson was also a member of the Texas Folklore Society in which Boatright was active. First printed in 1941 in the *Southwestern Social Science Quarterly,* the essay has been reprinted in Ernest B. Speck, ed., *Mody Boatright, Folklorist: A Collection of Essays* (Austin: University of Texas Press, 1973), pp. 13–38.

13. Boatright, "The American Myth Rides the Range," in Speck, *Mody Boatright,* pp. 80–91. Gipson regularly read and had often contributed stories to the *Southwest Review,* in which Boatright's essay first appeared in 1951. Beck Gipson, interview, Feb. 5, 1984.

14. Evan Thomas, in foreword to *Cowhand: The Story of a Working Cowboy,* by Fred Gipson (1948; College Station: Texas A&M University Press, 1977), p. vii. All subsequent citations from this edition will be given parenthetically in the text.

15. Tom Lea, quoted in Bennett, *Talking with Texas Writers,* p. 286.

16. My description is based on Nicholas J. Karolides, *The Pioneer in the American Novel, 1900–1950* (Norman: University of Oklahoma Press, 1964), chaps. 2–3.

17. Similarly threatened is Col. Zack Miller in *Fabulous Empire.* The modified argument from circumstance suggested by this threat is further developed in Schweizer's *Bauernroman und Faschimus.*

18. Claude Lévi-Strauss, *Myth and Meaning* (New York: Schocken, 1978), p. 38.

19. For insights into the ability of formulaic Hill Country tales to criticize domestic life, I am indebted to Minetta Altgelt Goyne (interview with author, Sept. 23, 1983) and to Ingeborg McCoy, "Tales the Grandmothers Tell," paper presented at the Lone Star and Eagle Symposium at the University of Houston, Sept. 25, 1983.

20. See Lévi-Strauss, *Myth and Meaning,* pp. 42–43.

21. The argument suggested here is developed in Mortimer, *Faulkner's Rhetoric of Loss,* pp. 43–71.

22. Lévi-Strauss, *The Savage Mind,* p. 21.
23. Compare Arnheim, "A Plea for Visual Thinking," p. 176.
24. See Meyer, *Middle Western Farm Novel.*

CHAPTER FIVE

1. Refer specifically to Joan Givner, *Katherine Anne Porter: A Life* (New York: Simon and Schuster, 1982), pp. 141–63. Without a doubt, part of the difference in "*The Cow Killers*" comes from the collaboration of Fred Gipson and Bill Leftwich. Leftwich apparently also assisted with aspects of the writing, particularly with helping Gipson hone the pictorial quality of the narrative texts. Bill Leftwich, telephone conversation with author, Sept. 16, 1984. See also Frank Wardlaw's foreword to Fred Gipson, "*The Cow Killers*": *With the Aftosa Commission in Mexico* (Austin: University of Texas Press, 1956), pp. vii–viii.

2. Gipson, "*The Cow Killers*", p. 4. All subsequent citations from this edition are given parenthetically in the text.

3. Thomas Beckton ("Beck") Gipson, interview with author, Apr. 1, 1984; Cox, *Fred Gipson,* pp. 168–69.

4. Fred Gipson, "The Roads Lead West," unpublished novel manuscript, quoted in Cox, *Fred Gipson,* p. 132.

5. Cox, *Fred Gipson,* pp. 140, 145; Gipson letter to Lyndon Johnson in Gipson Papers, Humanities Research Center, University of Texas at Austin.

6. The context of new world myths is studied most comprehensively in Frank E. Manuel and Fritzie P. Manuel, *Utopian Thought in the Western World* (Cambridge: Harvard University Press, 1979); for specific points applicable to Gipson's writing refer to Richard Slotkin, *Regeneration through Violence: The Mythology of the American Frontier, 1600–1860* (Middletown, Conn.: Wesleyan University Press, 1973) and Henry Nash Smith, *Virgin Land* (Cambridge: Harvard University Press, 1970). Furthermore, in line with Gipson's equation between land use and quality of life, see Richard Peet, ed., *Radical Geography: Alterna-*

tive Viewpoints on Contemporary Issues (Chicago: Maaroufa, 1977). *Radical Geography* contains particularly relevant chapters on behavioral geography, geographical warfare, and spatial planning that have no direct bearing on Gipson and his work but that inform what might have been his motivation toward preservation of a quality of life.

CHAPTER SIX

1. In his eulogy for Fred Gipson, Frank Wardlaw referred to comments by Walter Prescott Webb comparing Gipson's work "to that of Mark Twain in its universality of appeal to people of all ages and places" (Cox, *Fred Gipson,* pp. 194, 99). In the foreword to Cox's *Fred Gipson,* Joe Small similarly linked Gipson and Twain, saying "Fred Gipson could get into the very inside of a little boy and his dog perhaps as no other author ever has" (p. xx).

2. Fred Gipson, *The Trail-Driving Rooster* (New York: Harper, 1955), p. iii. All subsequent citations from this edition are given parenthetically in the text.

3. Leonard Maltin, *The Disney Films* (New York: Bonanza, 1973), pp. 145–46.

4. The two posthumous stories, or novelettes, are pure adventures, well-crafted but lacking in the characteristics one associates with Gipson's other works. My feeling is that Gipson would eventually have expanded these stories into novels more in the style of *Old Yeller* and *Savage Sam*—the process by which Gipson wove the stories of Recollection Creek into a novel and by which he probably wrote much of his fiction.

5. Compare C. Hugh Holman's comments on point of view and nostalgic longing, in *Windows on the World: Essays on American Social Fiction* (Knoxville: University of Tennessee Press, 1979), pp. 184–85.

6. Fred Gipson, quoted in Cox, *Fred Gipson,* pp. 136, 138, 169–70.

7. Cox, *Fred Gipson,* p. 160, and Mike Cox, interview with author, Feb. 11, 1984.

8. Fred Gipson, *Old Yeller* (New York: Harper, 1956), pp. 1, 2. All subsequent citations from this edition are given parenthetically in the text.

9. See Frantz, "Ethnicity and Politics in Texas," pp. 191–96. Amidst the controversy of secession, a separatist movement had once aimed toward establishment of a "State of West Texas." During the Civil War, when Federal troops were withdrawn from the frontier forts, the settlers were left to fend for themselves against bandits, Indians, and vigilantes.

10. In 1953, Fred and Tommie Gipson lost a newborn daughter (Cox, *Fred Gipson*, p. 126).

11. Gipson may not have remembered, and may never have known, when he chose his title, that yellow dogs were associated with bad luck and death. Refer to Jobes, *Dictionary of Mythology, Folklore, and Symbols.* Regarding Aaron Blood, see Henderson, *Fred Gipson*, p. 35.

12. Cox, *Fred Gipson*, pp. 158, 160–63; compare Morris Beja, *Film and Literature: An Introduction* (New York: Longman, 1979), chap. 4, for a concise discussion of principles of film adaptation based on novels. During the scripting and production of *Return of the Texan, Old Yeller,* and *Hound-Dog Man,* Gipson argued for realistic details, but he was slow to acquire an understanding for the film as a genre in its own right. By the time he wrote *Savage Sam,* however, he had learned basic principles of adaptation, and he applied cinematic techniques to his last major novel.

13. Maltin, *Disney Films,* pp. 145–46. The film collapses four episodes, during which a reader of the novel observes Travis's growth, into one composite event. And the film prolongs the final episode. Rather than recognizing the inevitability of the dog's contracting rabies after being bitten by a rabid animal, the Coates family in the film locks Old Yeller in a corncrib (admittedly the most memorable imagery in the film) and shoots him thus in confinement only after the dog succumbs to the final stages of the disease. The film evokes pathos, whereas the novel *uses* pathos to heighten the acquisition of a new, more powerful ethos. In the novel, Gipson spares the dog from an undignified death and ennobles Travis by requiring him, against all hope, to kill

a dog that looks healthy, shooting him one-on-one in the open rather than through the chinks of the corncrib.

14. Herman Lehmann (1859–1932) spent eight (not nine) years with Apaches and Comanches, eventually was adopted by Chief Quanah Parker, and as an Indian, was given Oklahoma lands by the federal government. Edited and published in 1927 by J. Marvin Hunter, Lehmann's *Nine Years among the Indians, 1870–1879* is the finest captive narrative in Texas literature. Both the book and Lehmann himself when he was in residence in the Hill Country were incredibly popular among residents of Mason and surrounding counties. A. C. Greene has written an adaptation, *The Last Captive* (1971). See A. C. Greene, "Herman Lehmann," in Branda, *Handbook of Texas*, 3:517.

15. Fred Gipson, *Savage Sam* (New York: Harper, 1962), p. v. All subsequent citations from this edition are given parenthetically in the text.

16. Maltin, *Disney Films*, p. 212.

17. Burn Sanderson figures by name and type in several Gipson novels. Like that of Blackie Scantling in *Hound-Dog Man*, his prototype is Charlie Sanders of Mason, a close friend of Fred Gipson's father. Fred Gipson maintained close ties with Sanders until the latter's death.

18. Henderson, *Fred Gipson*, p. 48.

19. Jean Jacques Rousseau, in his "Principles of Autobiography," writes of the need to "doubly paint" the soul, showing the person at the time of an event and, later, reflecting back on that time.

20. Henderson, *Fred Gipson*, p. 45.

21. Gipson's critics, Sam Henderson in particular, observed no final summation in *Savage Sam*, but Gipson was in a literary depression from which he thought he might never rise.

22. Maltin, *Disney Films*, p. 212.

23. Carl Moneyhon, interview with author, May 11, 1984.

24. Cox, *Fred Gipson*, pp. 178–79; see also p. 130.

25. See Gipson, *The Home Place*, p. 66.

26. Gipson, *Fabulous Empire*, pp. 409–10.

27. Ibid., p. 410.

28. See Cox, *Fred Gipson*, p. 130, where he describes Gipson's "gut-level lure to remote places, almost as if he were a part of them. [Gipson] was beginning to think that only in an area of primitive isolation did life have any real meaning." This was in 1954. Almost twenty years later, Gipson felt, again through Cox's sensitive eye, that "A man was lucky . . . if he did not get old enough to realize that 'the best of what was going to happen to him had already happened.' That was one of nature's cruelest jokes: The body went to hell, while the mind wanted to hold back and try again for something better. 'It was like a man was pushed backwards downhill, seeing the top getting farther from him, but always seeing it, always wishing he could go back'" (p. 189).

CHAPTER SEVEN

1. Compare Irwin, *Doubling and Incest*, p. 6; and Paul Ricoeur, *Interpretation Theory: Discourse and the Surplus of Meaning* (Fort Worth: Texas Christian University Press, 1976), pp. 53–54. Irwin elucidates Claude Lévi-Strauss on structures; in Irwin's words, "a structure is a virtual object whose shadow alone is real." Ricoeur describes the function of symbols: "[S]ymbol brings together two dimensions, . . . two universes, of discourse, one linguistic and the other of a nonlinguistic order."

2. Cornelia Meigs et al., *A Critical History of Children's Literature* (New York: Macmillan, 1953), pp. 4–5.

3. Cox, *Fred Gipson*, pp. 130, 181. At the entrance to Gipson's place his friend, Holmes Jenkins, put up a large wooden sign with "Recollection Creek" carefully lettered in western-style script. Years later, after Fred's death, Beck Gipson took the sign down, cut it in half, and on the back of one half made a new sign—with a new name for the place (Carolyn Cook Gipson, interview).

4. Gipson, *The Home Place*, p. 222.

5. See Yi-Fu Tuan, in *Topophilia: A Study of Environmental Perception, Attitudes, and Values* (Englewood Cliffs, N.J.: Prentice-Hall, 1974),

pp. 113–14, and in *Space and Place: The Perspective of Experience* (Minneapolis: University of Minnesota Press, 1977), pp. 149–51, which advance a principle of topophilia—the attachment of sentiment to place—and a bonding of homeland and ethos that seems particularly characteristic of Fred Gipson. See also Leonard Lutwack, *The Role of Place in Literature* (Syracuse, N.Y.: Syracuse University Press, 1984), for a lucid discussion of the rhetoric of place in literature, likewise applicable to Gipson.

6. See Mabel Major and T. M. Pearce, *Southwest Heritage: A Literary History with Bibliographies*, 3rd ed. (Albuquerque: University of New Mexico Press, 1972), pp. 15–16.

7. William H. Goetzmann, "Time's American Adventures: American Historians and Their Writing since 1776," *American Studies International* 19, no. 2 (1981): 33–39.

8. Gerald W. Haslam, *Western Writing* (Albuquerque: University of New Mexico Press, 1974), p. 5.

9. Cox, *Fred Gipson*, p. 184.

10. Doris Kearns, "Angles of Vision," in *Telling Lives*, p. 93.

11. Edward L. Ruhe, "Pastoral Paradigms and Displacements, with Some Proposals," *Survivals of Pastoral*, ed. Richard F. Hardin (Lawrence: University of Kansas Publications, 1979), p. 134.

12. Elroy Bode, *This Favored Place: The Texas Hill Country* (Bryan, Tex.: Shearer, 1983), p. 86.

13. John Graves, recorded in *The American Southwest: Cradle of Literary Art*, ed. Robert W. Walts (San Marcos: Southwest Texas State University, 1981), p. 16. In a letter to the author dated Mar. 8, 1984, Graves states: "I knew Fred and liked him and have always enjoyed his work without feeling a need to analyze it."

14. Compare Jay Gurian, *Western American Writing: Tradition and Promise* (Deland, Fla.: Everett Edwards, 1975), pp. v, 115–25.

15. E. L. Doctorow, "False Documents," *American Review* 26 (1977): 229.

Bibliography

PUBLICATION HISTORY OF WORKS BY FRED GIPSON

Fabulous Empire: Colonel Zack Miller's Story. Boston: Houghton Mifflin, 1946. Condensed in *Holiday,* September 19, 1946, pp. 65–80.

Hound-Dog Man. New York: Harper, 1949. Condensed in *Omnibook Magazine,* June, 1949, p. 104. New York: Permabooks, 1959. New York: Harper (Perennial Library), 1965. Lincoln: University of Nebraska Press, Bison Book, 1980. Film: Twentieth Century Fox, 1958. *Blackie, Frauen und Hunde,* Zurich: Diana, 1951. *La chasse de Noël,* Paris: Michel, 1956. *Texas No Ryoshi,* Tokyo: Shinkigen-sha, 1959. *Blackie, Frauen und Hunde,* Konstanz and Stuttgart: Diana, 1960. *Cacciatori in Erba,* Milan: Mursia, 1963.

The Home Place. New York: Harper, 1950. Chicago: People's Book Club, 1950. London: Michael Joseph, 1951. Condensed in *Philadelphia Bulletin* Book-of-the-Week (*The Sunday Bulletin*), April 29, 1951, p. 1. Serialized in *The Idaho Farmer,* beginning Oct. 16, 1952. Film: *The Return of the Texan,* Twentieth Century Fox, 1952.

Big Bend: A Homesteader's Story. With J. O. Langford. Austin: University of Texas Press, 1952. 2nd ed., rev., 1973.

Cowhand: The Story of a Working Cowboy. New York: Harper, 1953. New York: Bantam, 1958. 2nd ed., College Station: Texas A&M University Press, 1977.

Recollection Creek. New York: Harper, 1955. New York: Harper (rev. ed. for young people), 1959. New York: Dell, 1964.

The Trail-Driving Rooster. New York: Harper, 1955. Rpt. with an introduction by Glen E. Lich, Austin: Eakin, 1987.

"The Cow Killers": With the Aftosa Commission in Mexico. Drawings by Bill Leftwich. Austin: University of Texas Press, 1956. Rpt., Chelsea, Mich.: Bookcrafters, 1984.

Old Yeller. New York: Harper, 1956. Serialized in *Collier's,* June–July, 1956. Condensed in *Reader's Digest Condensed Books,* 1956. New York: Harper (large type edition), 1956. New York: Pocket Books, 1957. New York: Scholastic, 1957. New York: Pocket Books, 1962. New York: Harper, 1964. New York: Harper, 1966. Film: Walt Disney, 1958. *Fidèle vagabond,* Paris: Michel, 1958. *Gample Yeller,* Stockholm: Lindqvist, 1958. *Mi compañero gruñon,* San Sebastian: Dinor, 1958. *Fidèle vagabond,* Paris: Hachette, 1959. *Gamle Gule,* Copenhagen: Gyldendal, 1959. *Kiiroi Roken,* Tokyo: Shincho-sha, 1959. *Sein Freund Jello,* Gütersloh: Bertelsmann, 1959; Gütersloh: Mohn, 1960; Gütersloh: Mohn, 1961 (three printings). *Il mio amico Yeller,* Milan: Mursia & Corticelli, 1963. *Zrzoun,* Prague: SNDK, 1963. *Rakkerfanten,* Oslo: Aschenhoug, 1964. *Sein Freund Jello,* Ravensburg: Maier, 1966. *Gamle Gule,* 2nd ed., Copenhagen: Gyldendal, 1971. *İhtiyar sari,* Istanbul: Milliyet Yayin, 1973.

Savage Sam. New York: Harper, 1962. New York: Pocket Books, 1963. New York: Harper (Perennial Library), 1976. Film: Walt Disney, 1963. London: Hodder and Stoughton, 1962. *Gamle Gules Søn,* Copenhagen: Gyldendal, 1963. *Vilde Sam,* Stockholm: Lindqvist, 1963. *Sam, chien du Texas,* Paris: Hachette, 1964. *Der wilde Sam,* Gütersloh: Mohn, 1965. *Gamle Gules Søn,* 2nd ed., Copenhagen: Gyldendal, 1972.

Little Arliss. New York: Harper, 1978; Harper Trophy Book, 1980.

Curly and the Wild Boar. New York: Harper, 1979; Harper Trophy Book, 1980.

Before Old Yeller. Ed. C. Richard King. Burnet, Tex.: Eakin, 1980.

OTHER SOURCES

The Gipson Collection housed in the Humanities Research Center of the University of Texas at Austin is contained in thirty-nine large boxes. It dates from a donation in 1965 by the author, at the urging of R. Henderson Shuffler, and from a donation in 1973 by the author's surviving son, T. Beckton Gipson of Kerrville. An inventory of the Gipson Collection fills twelve single-spaced pages. This list is broken down into book manuscripts ("A Cowboy for to Be," 71 pp.; "The Devil to Pay," 223 pp.; "The Road Leads West," 331 pp. [1954]; "The Way of Jesse Gentry," 245 pp. [1951]); printed television- and screenplays; typed television- and screenplays; documents; unlisted matter (correspondence, reviews and criticism, letters from readers); story manuscripts; published stories; features; and miscellaneous.

Index

Fred Gipson at Work was composed into type on a Compugraphic digital phototypesetter in twelve point Janson with two points of spacing between the lines. Janson Italic was selected for display. The book was designed by Jim Billingsley, typeset by Metricomp, Inc., printed offset by Thomson-Shore, Inc., and bound by John H. Dekker & Sons, Inc. The paper on which this book is printed carries acid-free characteristics for an effective life of at least three hundred years.

TEXAS A&M UNIVERSITY PRESS : COLLEGE STATION